SCHOOLS COUNCIL WORKING PAPER 54

Arts and the adolescent

a curriculum study from the
Schools Council's Arts and
the Adolescent Project based
at the University of Exeter
Institute of Education (1968–72)

Malcolm Ross

Evans/Methuen Educational

First published 1975 for the Schools Council
by Evans Brothers Limited
Montague House, Russell Square, London WC1B 5BX
and Methuen Educational Limited
11 New Fetter Lane, London EC4P 4EE

Distributed in the US by Citation Press
Scholastic Magazines Inc., 50 West 44th Street
New York, NY 10036
and in Canada by Scholastic–TAB Publications Ltd
123 Newkirk Road
Richmond Hill, Ontario

ISBN 0 423 44490 5

Printed in Great Britain by
Richard Clay (The Chaucer Press) Ltd
Bungay, Suffolk

Acknowledgement

The Schools Council and the publishers are grateful to Faber and Faber Ltd and Harcourt Brace Jovanovich Inc., New York, for permission to reproduce the lines on p. 70 from 'East Coker' from *Four Quartets* by T. S. Eliot.

Contents

Preface

In revising this report for publication I have referred frequently to Robert Witkin's *The Intelligence of Feeling* (Heinemann Educational, 1974). He and I worked together very closely on the Schools Council's Arts and the Adolescent project, and both this report and his book are the outcome of our cooperation, and are complementary. I have attempted to explain why we chose our particular approach to the problems of curriculum development as we saw them, and to present our assessment of the possibilities and opportunities now open to teachers of the arts.

Writing in the industrial pages of *The Guardian* on 3 June 1971, Stephen Wearne had this to say in an article entitled 'The making of a project manager':

> A project is thus a transient means of effecting a lasting change. The process is impulsive . . . [project managers] are the agents of change. Their cycle of work is a period of intense activity, but hopefully short relative to the subsequent life of the product in use.

The Arts and the Adolescent curriculum study was completed in just four years. Although the original team is now involved in the dissemination and evaluation of the 'product', it was never our intention to institutionalize the project. It is now for arts teachers themselves to judge the value of our work and to use it to bring about such changes as they would like to see.

I. A curriculum study – the work of the project

> Art education in Great Britain is in a state of great confusion. Completely different ideals and methods of teaching prevail at the primary, secondary, technical and university levels. No one in political or professional authority seems to know how much importance should be attached to the subject – indeed, no one seems to know how to give the subject a precise definition that would show its relation to other subjects in the curriculum and permit its integration within the educational system as a whole.
>
> HERBERT READ

In autumn 1966 Peter Cox (Principal of Dartington College of Arts) gave a talk on the future of arts education to a group of teachers at Dillington House in Somerset. Among his audience was Joslyn Owen, Joint Secretary designate of the Schools Council. Both men already knew something of the findings of the Council's *Enquiry 1: Young School Leavers* to be published in 1968. The picture that the report would present of pupils' poor evaluation of their music, art and drama lessons was going to be disheartening to everyone interested in the arts in education. True, the report was exclusively concerned with boys and girls who had already made up their minds to leave school at the earliest legal opportunity – a fact that would be reflected in their general attitude towards school and that might be expected to manifest itself in terms of an overriding concern with the 'usefulness' of the curriculum and its particular relevance to future employment. However, it was felt that the results were likely to be seen as indicating attitudes and priorities of much more general prevalence. The report would serve to endorse what many had felt for a long time: that the arts were failing to attract a serious and enthusiastic response from the boys and girls in secondary schools. *Enquiry 1* (HMSO, 1968) did indeed jerk the long-standing malaise of arts education sharply into focus.

Since the University of Exeter Institute of Education had been invited by the Schools Council to suggest curriculum projects, Peter Cox put forward a proposal for a project in the arts which was to come within the terms of the RoSLA (raising of the school-leaving age) programme. At the time scarcely any research or development work on the arts curriculum was being undertaken. The Schools

7

Council approved a one-year feasibility study with a brief that reflected concern over the effectiveness and relevance of secondary-school arts teaching. The project was to address itself to three related questions:

a What materials and methods in the field of the arts are most likely to elicit a lively response among young people? The arts for this purpose being taken to include visual art, music, dance, drama, literature, film and photography.

b How do young people view their own involvement in the arts in school and out of school; how much connexion is there between these two forms of often disparate activity?

c How much connexion can be made, and how much transfer of interest is possible, between one art and another, and between the arts and other subjects in the curriculum?

It had been felt necessary to give the study some prospect of a positive outcome and to this end the spirit of integration had been invoked. Apart from attempting to account for the success of those teachers who were able to draw a lively response from their pupils, the project was concerned particularly to investigate the possibility of enlisting out-of-school interests in support of the school curriculum and of discovering some formula for bringing work in the different arts subjects into closer relationship both with each other and with the curriculum as a whole. The Council had made it clear that it would be prepared to back a longer project if the feasibility study seemed to justify it.

There were problems at the outset. The original plan entrusted the study to a working party of teachers, college and university lecturers, advisers and HMIs, to be served by a research assistant. An appointment was made but was never taken up. A second research assistant – a teacher – was given the job but she resigned after her first meeting with the working party in October 1967. The whole undertaking then hung fire for some months while various attempts were made to find an alternative approach. In spring 1968 the project's executive committee agreed to a revised organizational structure and I was seconded from Exeter University Institute of Education to run the project as its organizer. Peter Cox was to remain overall director, and the working party was to operate in an advisory role. And so, in September 1968 we were ready to make a fresh start.

It is perhaps worth pausing over these initial troubles for a moment because they underline some of the difficulties that were bound to face any curriculum project in the arts – difficulties that in this particular case threatened the whole enterprise and that were not entirely overcome by the organizational reshuffle. The working party had been unable to develop a common point of view or to formulate a coherent plan or method of work. Most of its discussions were pro-

8

tracted and all of them inconsequential. The frustration of the working party and its fundamental ineffectuality arose from the difficulty members had in communicating with each other. Though they frequently used the same words they soon became aware that they signified different things, and all attempts to establish common ground among the different arts in relation to their educational function failed. The group grew weary of itself and was unable to devise any very clear role for its research assistant who was to be dispatched to visit schools, youth clubs and arts centres and to 'report back'.

My first task was to widen rapidly my own personal experience of schools and of arts teaching and then to attempt to define the key problems with which the arts curriculum was confronted. If a three-year curriculum study were to start in the following September, then the feasibility 'year' would in practice have to be completed within a term. Three months were all that could be allowed for the initial survey and assessment of the situation, and for the formulation of proposals for the project proper.

During September, October and November I moved about the country talking with teachers, headteachers, boys and girls in schools and youth clubs, and to a handful of celebrities from whose experience I hoped to benefit. Wherever possible I collected evidence on a tape-recorder. From the celebrities I learned little. That was my own fault because at that stage I really did not know how they might best help me. I recall, with some embarrassment, a number of overtures made and tentative schemes of collaboration suggested to individuals and projects already operating in fields related to our own. All these early contacts were soon lost. Of critical importance, however, was my first-hand experience of the schools. It was important because the work suddenly became very real, and abstract problems assumed personal immediacy.

The working party met twice during that first term to consider my progress reports. In October I outlined my general impressions of the schools and clubs I had visited. I had interviewed a number of headteachers and they had told me how they saw the arts in education. The following is one of these interviews:

> Ah good morning Mr Ross, nice to see you. I've just been seeing these boys; now I'd much rather talk to my boys, you know, than talk to you. You'll forgive me saying that – that's what I'm here for – it's wonderful to have such a happy relationship with the children; they can come in here, you know, and see me at any time. Now these boys have been complaining to me about the way that they've been treated by the manager of Tesco's. They work in the evening there, and they've been doing three hours' work and getting two hours' pay for it. Well, I was able to sort that out for them. That's good. Yes, it's the children that count.

Now do sit down. The project you're doing, I'm all for this kind of thing, you know. We've got a very good school here; everything's going very well indeed. We like to think of ourselves as progressive. Oh yes, there's a great deal going on here, and I'm very pleased with everything that Mr Vincent's doing for instance. ['Vincent', whose work I had come to see, had accompanied me into the head's study.] A very lively man, and he does what he does with my entire backing and my gratitude. Well, you see me surrounded by papers, and telephones; perhaps you'd like to swop jobs! You're a lucky fellow, you know; I hope you appreciate it. How about sitting here for two or three days? Sorting out these forms and questionnaires and answering these letters for me? The only trouble of course, is running a place like this, it's all go, you know. You don't have time to stop. But still it's a good job, and it's a worth-while job, but I'm worried, you know, I'm worried about the way the education system's going. I'm shortly having to face the problem of operating a school with three fewer staff next year. We're short of money, short of space, and all the time the number of pupils is going up. I can think now of a French master up there with forty-one pupils in a room built for twenty-five, and he's got about fifteen textbooks. And there are boys doing geography in there, he has geography in the school without maps, no atlases of their own.

You ask me about what I'm going to do to meet the coming trials and stringencies. Well the most important thing is to maintain the morale and the health of my teachers. And this I intend to do. Well, there's a limit on how far we can be burdened. I had fifty-one students in here last year, and I have apparently got some six new probationary teachers. The 'Newtown' Department of Education has in its wisdom laid on a course for probationary teachers, and I have written to tell them that I am only too delighted that my probationary teachers should do some further training. Have the chance of talking to people other than myself about the problems that arise – naturally I'm always available for them to talk to. However, I can't release six teachers. It means having six classes unattended. If they like to give me six members of their staff, then I'll be glad to cooperate with them. You see, Mr Ross, I'm all for progress and development, I see the value of training and of research and projects like yours but we have to get our priorities right.

Now, in the system such as ours, we're not free to do as we like. The examinations, now – whether we like it or not – these are the things that matter. My life is regulated by the GCE. Of course the CSE is all right in its way, but of course it's another burden, it's another . . . cross, another trial we have to meet. Everybody who comes here wants GCEs. The parents want the GCEs, the staff want the GCEs and I am afraid I cannot do just what I like. This wonderful work that Mr Vincent is doing . . . ['Vincent' had just returned from a year's drama course.] It's all very well, and I am only too delighted to give him what support I can, but this isn't a primary school you know and we have to get down to business. And soon. Now you must forgive me. Do call on Mr Vincent just whenever you like. We're very proud of him here.

There was no denying he had a point (even several) – no need of course to describe the conditions under which 'Vincent' was trying to utilize his new expertise. I did not always fare as badly as that.

Here for instance is an extract from an interview I had with the headmaster of a boys' secondary modern school:

I rate the importance of the arts in education very highly. Actively, the arts offer the average child an opportunity of self-expression and of spiritual satisfaction, of the release of emotional tensions; receptively the appreciation of art gives a stimulus to thought and deeper contemplation.

What impact do the arts make upon the life of your school?

A very considerable one – probably greater than inter-school games.

What do the arts mean to you personally?

Music and literature are of overwhelming importance to me.

What proportion of school time do you allow for the teaching of the arts in the fourth and fifth years?

More than ten per cent – although some of this has to be optional. All the music and much of drama and photography is extracurricular for fourth and fifth years. For example, the school orchestra practices every break and every lunchtime and two evenings per week. We are at present rather handicapped in that one or two valuable arts activities have no master eager and hard-working enough to foster them in the school but, as far as I am concerned, the arts have equal status with the academic subjects of the curriculum. Many of our better boys have stayed a sixth year and gone straight to the College of Art, and one to the Royal Academy of Music.

What qualities do you look for when appointing an arts teacher?

Teaching ability and an enthusiasm for his art that is infectious – but without eccentricities of appearance and manner.

How easy is it to find the right kind of teachers?

11

It is very, very difficult. I think it is vitally important to keep up a high standard – certainly in what we introduce to the children. For most of them the school will be their only means of coming into contact with anything that is truly great art. Except occasionally – for comparative and discussion purposes – there is no time in school to devote to commercial 'pop' music, strip cartoons, etc. The pupils are spoonfed with this in enormous quantities anyway. It is the task of a school to lead the pupils towards real art. To say that the only difference between Mozart and the Monkees is one of personal taste between equals is just not true and it smacks of humbug to curry favour with the young. That here we find sixty or seventy boys willing to pay to go to an orchestral concert I consider very satisfactory.

In this particular school there was one full-time art master and no full-time teacher of music or drama. The head handled much of the school's musical appreciation himself – it was clearly something to which he attached considerable importance. His general attitude was echoed by many of the headteachers I spoke to: here was a sincere commitment to the idea of the expressive and civilizing function of the arts wedded to a determination to hold out for high standards. It is just possible, however, that his own strong views might have militated against his recruiting further arts staff, for he makes a number of assumptions that at least some teachers would want to challenge. If one were attempting to revise or expand the teaching of the arts in his school it would seem entirely pointless to take him to one side and to argue the case for arts education. He was already convinced. But, ironically, his very convictions might prove to be a major factor blocking radical curriculum reform.

That some of the assumptions commonly made about arts education needed challenging now became clear. The heads seemed to have distinctly limited ideas about the function of the arts in education: although many of them genuinely felt that the arts had a part to play and felt impelled to support the efforts of their arts teachers, in practice they were inclined to treat the arts as valuable spare-time activities, as useful for special occasions, or simply as service departments. The heads were generally very aware of the difficulties created for their staff by the timetable and by unsuitable buildings and inadequate resources, but they seemed powerless to alleviate them, and, in view of their general endorsement of the public examination system, tended to accept that they were unalterable. There was a widespread assumption that, beyond the first two or three years, the brighter boys and girls could not afford to give time to the arts but that there might be something in music, art or drama lessons for the slower streams and the more difficult individuals.

The most striking feature of my discussions with arts teachers was their

12

vagueness and confusion when pressed on the questions of immediate educational goals and long-term objectives. There appeared to be no general agreement among them concerning their own function in relation to their pupils, or of the function of the arts in the educational process. A natural consequence was their anxiety over the whole question of validation – of their own work and of that of their pupils. Many complained of being held in little professional esteem by the staff as a whole, and all gave the impression of working lives lived in some degree of isolation. Few of them had any clearly developed ideas about either integrating the arts or about connecting with the real lives of their adolescent pupils.

The pupils I spoke to had their own reasons for liking or disliking their schools. There were of course many satisfied clients. There were many more who were prepared to 'string along'. (I found the greatest apathy in the grammar schools I visited.) However, it was difficult to avoid sensing the waste of human potential on a considerable scale. It was almost as if school had been especially designed to frustrate the natural processes of education and to cripple in the young the strong drives that, in different circumstances, might make learning as self-propelled and as self-rewarding as it was instinctive. As for the arts, '. . . well, they weren't of any particular use to you but they could be fun'. My own experience confirmed the width of the gap, described in *Enquiry 1*, between the values of the pupils and those of the teachers. However, it was beginning to occur to me that – although this gap unquestionably existed – it represented a frustration somewhat different from that suggested by the Schools Council survey. The allegedly impractical ideals of the teachers seemed to have little impact upon the shape of a curriculum that was experienced by the pupils not only as irrelevant (i.e. too 'academic') but also, perhaps more significantly, as dreary and repressive. The teachers had to insist that, although in an ideal world school might have been different, in practice they had no choice over the style and content of education. Some of the pupils complied some of the time – but many of those I talked with, particularly in 'non-academic' classes, were demanding a quite different experience: one that was marked by a sense of applicability to the needs they felt and that offered a chance of real participation. In our schools research we came eventually to probe the pupils' conception of the curriculum fairly intensively. In terms of pupil response the basic curriculum problem seemed to be to tie enjoyment and a sense of personal satisfaction with task esteem and the conviction that what one was doing really mattered. Both the teachers and the pupils seemed to be trapped in a relationship that each resented and that neither was able to change.

When we were testing a pupil questionnaire some time later, we received the following unsolicited comments from a fourth-year secondary-modern girl. (She

13

was asked her father's job and had written down, 'Self-employed, farmer. STILL ALIVE NO LONGER WITH US.'):

Art: This is not as it should be but very enjoyable.

English: Not what it should be, very boring and certainly not interesting.

Music: Music is boring. The so-called music is so boring we just feel like sleeping and as for having a say in what we do we don't have any decent records. We are not expecting to have pop records all the time but we could at least have a choice.

Needlecraft: This is also very boring.

Drama: This is the only lesson where we have a say in school affairs. We have a very nice teacher, we should have more *lessons* and *teachers* like this.

In December I again reported to the working party, dealing with each of the project's terms of reference in turn in an attempt to reduce the profusion of experience to some order. I had seen some 'lively' teaching of music, art and drama, but it was going to be very difficult to deduce cause from effect. Different teachers adopted widely differing approaches. The military style of one art teacher ('Johnson will issue the pencils: I have personally sharpened them all, so God help the laddie who breaks one!'), brought cheerful cooperation from his class of 13-year-olds, perhaps not least because the class exercises he set them were well within everyone's competence. These boys moved through the arts curriculum guided by an explicit set of rewards and punishments that they well understood and that the teacher fairly administered. The talented ones among them were allowed special treatment and worked in the teacher's own small study; the less gifted recognized the propriety of this arrangement. In most obvious respects the art lesson was like any school lesson except that it was probably more fun than most of them.

In a different school, when I entered the art room I had difficulty discerning the art teacher at all. The scene was not a little confusing: a jumble of junk, paper, a huge press, tables, pots, books and 'found objects'. The teacher – young, bearded and self-effacing – was bending over his own work in a far corner. Twenty 14-year-old boys and girls were busy – some on their own, some in groups of two or three – on a wide range of projects. There was no laughter, no spirited chatter, no apparent excitement, and yet the sense of engagement was very strong and the detached expressions that I saw on some of the faces in that class suggested secret and intense inner activity. In fact, as the weeks went by, I came gradually rather to distrust classes full of over-excitement and bright faces. I learned to look for other signs that might distinguish the engagement of

14

adolescent boys and girls from that of younger children. I came to find the term 'lively response' less and less helpful as a criterion by which to assess the quality of a lesson.

The situation described in the following extract taken from my field notes illustrates yet another approach: one in which the teacher must have felt he had gone as far as he could to reach his pupils.

> In one of the art rooms a young teacher was only barely keeping control. He was taking a class called V Building and there were some eight or nine hefty 15-year-old boys sitting around in casual attitudes with drawing boards perched on their knees. They were making desultory attempts at drawing a large motor-bike that the teacher had stationed in the centre of the room. The head of the department, who was taking me round, said 'They love drawing things like that.' The boys were loud and truculent. The teacher looked hunted, as he plied rapidly from one boy to the next making no real contact with any of them. He was clearly embarrassed by our intrusion and one could not blame him.

Two important points had emerged for the project from these early attempts to understand what was happening in the schools. First, we would have to study arts teaching much more closely – and we would need some specialized help in preparing the instruments and developing the methods appropriate to such a study. For only when we were able to present the curriculum in a form that would permit detailed analysis and comparison would we be in a position to assess the appropriateness and effectiveness of a teacher's work or determine a proper basis for any future change. Secondly, we had become convinced that the curriculum had to be developed from the inside – that is to say that learning had to spring from the unique experience of a teacher and his or her pupils, that the motivation of all of the participants was a key determinant of learning efficiency and that, provided those involved in the situation could behave authentically (and this, of course, is a factor of personal relationships), then considerable flexibility of teaching style and approach was to be expected and indeed welcomed in the classroom. The urgently needed consensus over aims and objectives should not preclude considerable diversity of curriculum content and method.

My inquiries in connexion with the two remaining terms of reference yielded rather less as a basis for further study. The widespread assumption, for instance, that pop music and pop culture were of burning importance to the majority of teenagers was simply not borne out in the discussions I had had. The enthusiastic chart-watchers and star-gazers tended to be the younger boys and girls. The older ones certainly expressed a strong preference for their own style of music but there were many more pressing issues that exercised their thoughts and feelings. Among boys and girls at school I found little of the commitment to pop values or a pop life-style sometimes to be found among sections of older students or undergraduates. Attempts to resuscitate school music or school art by transfusions from the pop scene or the brash world of the mass media were usually abortive, resulting merely in the revamping of the music lesson in a *Top of the Pops* format or the production of trendy school magazines and derivative art work. No one was impressed – least of all the pupils.

I discovered very few successful instances of continuity of experience between primary and secondary schools, or of continuity of provision between the schools, youth clubs and colleges of further education. The particular arts clubs and arts workshops that I visited seemed to attract mostly, though certainly not exclusively, middle-class children from homes in which the arts were already actively supported. And as far as 'integration' was concerned I found that, even when teachers felt they understood why, few of them pretended to know how to achieve effective collaboration with other arts teachers or between arts teachers and colleagues from other departments. It seemed to me that, among the factors militating against the emulation by secondary teachers of the happy examples set by some primary schools, two stood out – the demands of external examinations and the career structure within the profession – both of which were important instances of curriculum determined by external constraints.

A pattern was now discernible among the impressions I had gathered. Many teachers and pupils seemed to find the schools frustrating and diminishing in varying degrees. Some of the teachers I had spoken to had been forced to make distasteful compromises that meant relinquishing the very ideals that nourished their creative work and informed their sense of human relationships – of being human. Pupils were frequently held down in dependent and passive roles when their burgeoning faculties demanded greater participation and greater personal responsibility for their own lives: their real questions were not being listened to nor their real demands met. For some, frustrated energy usually found expression – owing to lack of scope or opportunity – in frivolous or disruptive diversions. There were others, of course, who merely switched off, who withdrew into real or assumed indifference. In this depressing context the arts lesson often stood out like an oasis in a desert. Arts lessons were usually fun, and the relaxed and friendly atmosphere, the direct and personal relationships that frequently characterized them, meant that I met few pupils who wished to drop the arts and many who regretted having to give up these subjects or to choose between them. Of course, the arts subjects were not 'important' and doing art or drama or music was not 'work', but most of the girls and boys I spoke to looked forward to these lessons and for one or two children in every school the particular relationship with an arts teacher was essential to their basic stability and to their functioning in the school at all. As 'time off' the arts were doing a useful job. Apart from that, arts teachers might be relied upon to recognize the talented individual and to encourage his or her development.

But the question remained, was such an account of the purpose and value of arts education enough? Did it do justice to the teachers' ideals or even to their actual practice? The answer on both counts had to be 'no'. In any case, the concern of the project was not with the gifted few but with the more modestly endowed many. We were asking what was wrong with the way the arts functioned within the concept of a general education. Many teachers – some arts teachers – felt that this was hardly a question of the first importance. There was, for instance, a strong voice among music teachers advocating dropping music from the general curriculum altogether, but this I took to be a desperate remedy for what was perceived as a desperate situation, and most of the music teachers I met would have nothing to do with it. The music teacher who felt that the 'unmusical' were best employed painting the music stands was unique in my experience. Music teachers soldier on in the classroom because they are convinced that music plays a key role in human experience and that, as such, it has an important contribution to make to a humane education.

The same can of course be said of the arts as a whole. Without such a conviction nothing would be achieved, but of itself it is not enough; an effective curriculum cannot be built upon blind conviction. Watching arts teachers at work, I was aware of great ingenuity, great resourcefulness and often superhuman commitment in circumstances that I found not simply trying but entirely baffling. I was also aware that the quality of the experience in which teachers and pupils shared seemed to vary alarmingly: some classes seemed to be doing little more than amiably passing the time; in others the pupils were being rigorously drilled into making the responses that were expected of them. In some classes one experienced a sense of engagement and quiet purpose; in others mere excitement and muddle. When asked about their aims and their general understanding of their own educational function most of the arts teachers I spoke to were either struck totally dumb or rapidly collapsed into incoherence. It was not that they had no sense of where they were going or of what they were doing – rather that their own best work seemed to derive more from intuition than deliberation and, although they insisted that in some respects they were concerned with areas of experience not easily expressed in words, they none the less remained uneasy about their inarticulateness and felt that somehow it should be possible to say what arts education was about and why it was important.

Here, then, were the questions to which we had to address ourselves. In the finding of adequate answers lay our chance of contributing to the future

17

development of arts education. It seemed to me that no good whatever was to come from the kind of approach implied in the original terms of reference, all of which made the assumption that the quality of the arts lesson could be affected and improved extrinsically by the manipulation of external circumstances or the deployment of material resources, by trying to make school like out-of-school or persuading one teacher to imitate another. It became for us an article of faith that a teacher's salvation lay in his own hands – in being not less true but more true to himself, in understanding what he was doing, assessing it and redesigning his work to meet his own continually evolving sense of purpose. His salvation – and that of arts education – lay in having not less but more direct control over what he did. Given this greater understanding and greater control, we already had entirely adequate human resources to make the arts the vital force that we sensed they had to be if education were really to promote what Norbert Weiner calls 'the human use of human beings'.

I concluded my second report to the working party by suggesting that it was now necessary radically to realign and refocus the project's effort. Our aim should be: 'To offer a rationale for the place of the arts in secondary education so as to assist teachers and others to discriminate between the aims which should receive particular emphasis in the building of a new curriculum.' We should make our study as scientific as possible and, while giving attention to the questions 'What should we teach?' and 'How should we teach it?', our first concern should be to seek an answer to two much more fundamental questions: 'What do we mean by arts education?' and 'Why teach the arts in school anyway?'

That is what had to be done. There was simply no point in attempting anything less, and so I prepared a three-year plan which was submitted to the Schools Council in January 1969. In essence my suggestion was that the proposed project should attempt an intensive study of the arts curriculum of some six secondary schools, selected in the first instance on the strength of their arts departments. Each department would be researched in the first year and in particular would be asked to define its aims and objectives. Then, in consultation with and supported by the project, the schools would develop their own experimental arts curricula. The project would set out to monitor, record and evaluate each piece of action research in the hope that certain basic principles might emerge and that these, together with a record of the whole process of curriculum development, might offer insights and guidelines for others. It must be said that I had some misgivings about the proposal and that my own uneasiness was shared by members of the project's executive committee who doubted that I had been sufficiently explicit.

Then, on 4 February 1969, Robert Witkin and I happened to meet in Exeter.

We began to discuss the project and together we rapidly sketched out the details of a programme of three years' work – a programme that had a clear connexion with the feasibility study, but which now included a more credible and more explicit plan of action. It was organic in conception and involved the concurrent and interrelated development of a conceptual framework and of a programme of empirical research. This notion of interrelatedness was critical to the new project's method, since the research would be designed in terms of a conceptual framework and the research findings would be instrumental in its modification. In the final product (the form of which was not yet determined) conception and research were to be completely interwoven. It was to be conceived not as a report or a tract, but as an activator – a probe into consciousness.

When I met the Schools Council to discuss the proposal I was able to offer them the prospect of a language which would enable arts teachers better to understand and control their work: a language that would have to be equally applicable to all the arts. This language would emerge as part of a more far-reaching study of the educational function of the arts based upon original work in the psychology of affect, on which Robert Witkin was already engaged. It was just possible that, over and above the 'language', the Council would be offered a work of fundamental significance to education generally, perhaps to be called *The Intelligence of Feeling*. No promises could be made. The decision to go ahead would inevitably be something of a gamble. In March 1969 the Schools Council approved the study.

This decision was of course crucial; it was also bold. It was a commitment to ideas rather than to plans. Perhaps such a decision could only have been taken at that particular moment in the Schools Council's history. Since that time there has been a gradual clarifying of the different and complementary roles of the Schools Council and the Social Science Research Council, with the latter eschewing altogether the applied field. The Schools Council, continuing to maintain its own research team and to commission research work, has none the less developed an increasingly activist policy characterized most typically by direct intervention in the schools through the devising and publication of curriculum materials. While it is certainly true that in March 1969 some element of practical experiment in schools formed an explicit part of the project's plans, it was clear from the very outset and manifest in its descriptive title that this project, a 'curriculum study', would be difficult to classify in terms of the Council's major divisions of work. And so it has remained right up to the completion of the project. It was neither proposed nor demanded of us that the project produce curriculum materials. Nor were we ever simply engaged upon pure research. Our intention was always to intervene – to activate change – but our approach was to be a somewhat unfamiliar one. We wished to bring about change in the arts

19

curriculum indirectly, by facilitating thinking and disseminating ideas. Our work would in large measure draw upon and be addressed to the consciousness of arts teachers. Our method, as already described, would be to study arts teaching and to develop an instrument which would enable arts teachers themselves to control the future of arts education.

The Schools Council invested £40 000* in the wholly unpredictable field of conceptual speculation and exploration. Their judgement rested upon an estimation of the likelihood of particular minds bringing a promising idea to fruition – this is entirely different from putting someone under contract to produce copies of a model already developed or to test and develop a revised version. The principles implicit in this decision are that the outcome of certain types of investigation cannot be predetermined, that maximum flexibility of method must be allowed (that is, that the development be evolutionary rather than mechanical), and that in some circumstances people make better investments than programmes. The Council had the flimsiest of evidence and no definable product to anticipate. A detailed account of the project's work would reveal a process of continuous and frequently painful adjustment and reorganization as the team pursued their elusive quarry with whatever resources they could muster, given the constraints within which they were committed to operate. As in Marvell's poem, anxiety levels could run very high: Time's wingèd chariot always seemed on the point of overhauling us.

In such circumstances it was invaluable to have the regular cycle of meetings with the project's consultative committee. Progress reports had to be prepared and stock taken. Work of this kind exerts its own strain and calls for a rather special kind of support. Whatever we may have achieved in the end has in some measure grown out of the faith originally placed in us by the Schools Council and owes much to the 'resistance' provided by our consultative committee. It would be a pity if the Council were less venturesome in the future; less free to act with vision and courage when education continues to need both.

The feasibility study had shown that many arts teachers were working in distinctly unsympathetic circumstances. Their difficulties in the classroom, however, seemed to arise, at least in part, from their own confusion over their role and over the educational function of their subjects. The project's original terms of reference were based upon a set of naive assumptions about curriculum development and were unlikely to give rise to an adequate understanding of the functioning of the arts curriculum. A rather special kind of research project with a limited and sharply focused set of objectives was needed. The main aim of such a project would be to construct a basic conceptual framework which would permit the analysis and assessment of current practice and provide a proper foundation for

* The total cost of the four years' work was in the region of £45 000.

controlled experiment. With the recruitment of Robert Witkin as Research Director this was the task which we were now able to undertake.

The schools research and work on the conceptual framework proceeded simultaneously. It would be difficult for me to attempt to trace the development of the conceptual framework during the course of the project. I would simply say that being close to that development was invariably an exhilarating and occasionally rather an awesome experience. The schools research is rather a different matter and I shall first quote from a paper in which Robert Witkin outlined the research programme for a meeting of the consultative committee in December 1970:

> Our central concern is to learn about the nature and operation of the arts programmes in schools. This is the detailed research designed to feed the project with essential information about what takes place in arts lessons and why, about the priorities, interests and attitudes of arts teachers and of pupils, about the place of the arts in our schools and in the lives of the children and finally about the formal structure of the school, methods of teaching and their comparative effectiveness. We have selected six rather varied types of school for the [schools] research and hope to provide as full a description as possible of each of these schools with regard to the factors in which we are interested.
>
> The research instruments to be employed are as follows:
>
> a   Observations of arts lessons
> b   Pupil questionnaire (all pupils)
> c   Staff questionnaire (all staff)
> d   Pupil interview (selected sample)
> e   Staff interview (all arts teachers)
> f   Creativity test (pupils selected for interview)
> g   Jack Walton's Curriculum Notation System (for producing curriculum analysis)
> h   Pupil assessment scale (teachers' evaluation of pupil interview sample)
> i   Teacher activities proforma (outline of teaching activities).
>
> We shall spend two weeks in each school and will, in addition to the formal instruments, employ informal techniques to gather further background information relevant to the arts within the locale of the school.

The schools research was conducted in three consecutive phases: preparation, fieldwork and data processing. After the necessary preliminary correspondence, each school was visited by a member of the team to discuss details of the research timetable and of the administrative arrangements (timetables, numbers of pupils in each form, streaming, accommodation, etc.). Pupil questionnaires were sent to the school in advance of the research fortnight, administered by the teachers and returned to us for preliminary coding and analysis – on the basis of which the sample of children for more intensive study (creativity testing and interviewing) was drawn. Pupils were chosen either because their interests were very strongly aligned with the arts or because they showed a strong orientation to some other area of the curriculum. They were interviewed in homogeneous groups of three or four. During the six research fortnights we administered the Torrance Creativity Test* to a 10 per cent sample of the total pupil population, we tape-recorded 201 interviews with 467 pupils; 107 arts lessons were observed and described in written reports; interviews with 57 arts teachers were taped; 288 teacher questionnaires were distributed and 151 completed. In addition to all this, Jack Walton of Exeter University Institute of Education spent several days annotating and analysing each school's timetable to provide us with the information that would help us grasp the 'message' of each curriculum, to compare one school with another and to contrast what the pupils said they wanted with what the school actually provided. General background information about each school was collected informally.

As each fortnight's work was completed the process of data analysis began. In all, some 4435 pupil questionnaires were coded and punched on to cards. Most of this material was analysed by computer and descriptive diagrams were produced from computer print-outs. The teacher questionnaires and Torrance Tests were also coded and punched onto cards but were not, in the event, analysed. The interviews with the teachers were all transcribed. Content analysis of the pupil interviews was undertaken and a selected sample transcribed. This complex and time-consuming operation was still going on at the time of writing. The problem has lain in 'playing' the results: in deciding which data to work on and which to put aside; in making an interpretation of the results and then finding some means of checking; ultimately, in discerning a pattern among the disparate parts and judging how to deploy the 'findings' in support of the 'idea'.

Simultaneously with the main programme of work on its twin fronts of conceptualization and empirical research, the project was gradually accumulating information of a different kind and for a rather different purpose. Recognizing the necessarily narrow focus and limited range of the schools research, we felt we had to build, from any available sources, a more general picture of the state of arts education so that we might be able to put our own research findings into perspective. If it were true that arts education was sick, then we had to look

* See E. P. Torrance, *Guiding Creative Talent* (Prentice-Hall, Englewood Cliffs, New Jersey, 1962).

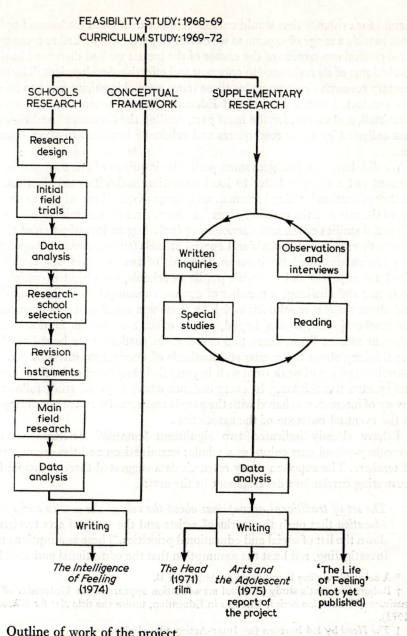

FEASIBILITY STUDY: 1968-69
CURRICULUM STUDY: 1969-72

SCHOOLS   CONCEPTUAL   SUPPLEMENTARY
RESEARCH   FRAMEWORK   RESEARCH

Research design

Initial field trials

Data analysis

Research-school selection

Revision of instruments

Main field research

Data analysis

Written inquiries

Observations and interviews

Special studies

Reading

Data analysis

Writing

Writing

The Intelligence of Feeling (1974)

The Head (1971) film

Arts and the Adolescent (1975) report of the project

'The Life of Feeling' (not yet published)

Fig. 1 Outline of work of the project.

23

around for evidence that would corroborate our own and take 'second opinions' from as wide a range of experts as we could. In particular we had to come up with some general assessment of the causes of the inertia we had discerned in the arts curriculum: of its resistance to coherent and effective development. The supplementary research programme, as these more general inquiries came to be called, was conducted at the Institute of Education as and when time and resources permitted, and meant, for the most part, reading the literature* and re-working data collected by other researchers and originally intended to serve other purposes.

We did, however, instigate some particular inquiries of our own: for instance, we sent out a circular letter to local education authorities and institutions of teacher education inviting comment on a range of questions related to the teaching of the arts and the training of arts teachers. And we commissioned a number of special studies of the arts curriculum† including an investigation of the work of arts therapists in hospitals and special schools (summarized as Appendix A). In addition we asked Ed Berman, Director of Inter-Action Trust, to make a film‡ for experimental use with pupils in schools, the object of which would be to test and challenge a number of common assumptions both about the arts and about the arts in schools; and John Lane was asked to devise a source book for teachers§ that, it was hoped, would effect a somewhat similar result by different means. From these two exercises in particular we hoped to sharpen our thinking about the means and methods of curriculum intervention. In the event both pieces of work went well beyond their brief and embodied important and constructive thinking. In every instance where a special study followed discovery of interests we shared with the people concerned we were not disappointed in the eventual outcome of the association.

I have already indicated two significant 'external' determinants of the secondary-school curriculum as a whole: examinations and the career structure of teachers. The supplementary research data suggested three principal factors frustrating curriculum development in the arts:

a   *The set of traditional assumptions about the role of the arts in society and in education* that push the works of artists and the work of arts teachers well down the list of social and educational priorities. These assumptions needed investigating, not least the assumption that the educational and social func-

* A selected reading list appears as Appendix B.
    † Robert Clement's study of visual art education appears in the University of Exeter Institute of Education series, Themes in Education, under the title *Art for Whose Sake?* (1972).
    ‡ *The Head* by Ed Berman (an Inter-Action film, 1971).
    § 'The Life of Feeling', an anthology by John Lane (not yet published).

24

tions of the arts were identical. Expressed perhaps rather crudely, the fine arts are equated with the finer feelings, and artistic expression and patronage are seen as useless but characteristic appendages of the civilized way of life.

b   *The feeling that arts teachers are 'different'* – that, by virtue of their training and of the frivolous and mysterious nature of their work they cannot lay claim either to equality of status with colleagues whose backgrounds and preoccupations are academic, or to equality of function with the humble but honest artisan. Their influence upon the shape of the total curriculum was therefore likely to be distinctly limited.

c   *The crossed purposes of the arts curriculum today* – the lack of a pervading consensus. Arts teachers have turned under the big boot of academic tradition and turned again, with the result that many of them are now thoroughly dismayed. The flight from feeling, from the one field of experience with which the arts are uniquely concerned, is gathering momentum: arts teachers have for some time been in retreat before the academic tradition, in particular they are seeking to authorize their work in terms of the traditional examination system and by laying claim to often questionable goals.

Each of these problems is featured in the findings of our schools research and discussed in Robert Witkin's *The Intelligence of Feeling* (Heinemann Educational, 1974). I discuss them in more general terms in the next chapter of this report and, having done so, proceed to explain the particular approach we chose in an effort to support the teachers of the arts in schools.

II. The arts in secondary education
– a traditional role

While our main research effort went into preparing and carrying through the field work in our six research schools and then into processing and analysing the data we had collected we were also studying carefully a number of key documents which we hoped would provide an appropriate background against which the findings of our empirical research programme could be set. In particular we wished to learn something about the historical development of arts education: about the ways in which the educational function of the arts had been understood and had changed over the years. We wished to investigate the relationship between their perceived role and actual status in terms of provision and support, for it was already clear to us that the two were likely to be intimately connected. If, as we suspected, the arts had always been on the periphery of the school curriculum then we would expect the cause to lie in misconceptions about the essential purposes of arts education. We decided to look at the educational reports to see what kind of a picture they presented and to examine what they meant by an arts education. We then took the most recent set of DES statistics and learnt from them what we could of the current status of arts education – we looked at the ways in which the schools spent their time and money and how they deployed their teachers. We also felt it might be instructive to look at the special characteristics of an arts teacher's training and qualifications, on the assumption that they might in their turn have an important if indirect bearing on the effectiveness of the arts curriculum.

What the reports say

All the major reports from Hadow (1926)* to Newsom (1963)† speak of the powerful educational potential of the arts. In 1938 the Spens Committee‡ found

* Board of Education, *The Education of the Adolescent* [The Hadow Report, 1926] (HMSO, 1926).
† Central Advisory Council for Education (England), *Half our Future* [The Newsom Report] (HMSO, 1963).
‡ Board of Education, *Secondary Education with Special Reference to Grammar and Technical Schools* [The Spens Report] (HMSO, 1938).

26

it 'the gravest defect of the present system' that boys and girls could complete their secondary education having made virtually no contact 'with the tradition of the arts and crafts'. The report recommended that 'a more prominent and established place in the ordinary curricula of schools . . . should be assigned to the aesthetic subjects'. Norwood (1943)* complained similarly that the arts 'have not received the attention in schools which is due to them . . . These subjects too often are regarded as "special" when the one thing required is that they should be regarded as normal subjects'. McNair (1944)† felt that the arts in secondary schools needed encouragement and asked that every opportunity be given to 'artists and craftsmen of proved competence to enter the teaching profession'.

The Crowther Report (1959)‡ maintained that 'most 15-year-olds . . . need to be introduced to the arts and given the opportunity to practise them. These are not the flowers but the roots of education'. Faced with evidence of the way in which the arts were being squeezed out of the curriculum, the report insisted:

> If we regard the development of some pride of workmanship and some aesthetic sensibility as an important part of general education and one that is not finished by 13 or 14, we clearly cannot be content to leave it, in day schools, to after-school voluntary societies.

We might not be altogether satisfied with the Crowther Committee's sense of the aims of arts education but there can be no doubt that the report was right to demand that the arts be given their due in the formal curriculum. The point may be of less account today, when in many of our schools the distinction between curricular and extracurricular activity has less meaning, nevertheless – however constituted or defined – the serious educative responsibilities of a school cannot be properly discharged if the arts curriculum is regarded as largely irrelevant.

The arts subjects, according to the Newsom Report, 'offer creative and civilizing influences beneficial to all pupils'. It goes on to speak of 'an intense creative satisfaction in making and doing which is especially important for those who do not easily achieve expression in words: art, drama and dance, particularly, draw powerfully on feeling and provide both an emotional release and a channel through which feelings can be constructively employed'. And yet only half the schools studied by the committee had adequate accommodation for art, and less than a quarter had a proper music room. Having demonstrated that, where

* Board of Education, *Curriculum and Examinations in Secondary Schools* [The Norwood Report] (HMSO, 1943).

† Board of Education, *Teachers and Youth Leaders* [The McNair Report] (HMSO, 1944).

‡ Ministry of Education, *15 to 18* [The Crowther Report] (HMSO, 1959).

music in particular was concerned, 'some schools are being asked the near impossible' the report insists that the subject 'deserves generous encouragement'.

Norwood suggested a number of reasons why the arts subjects were undervalued and ill-provided for:

> Art, music and handicrafts . . . have not received the attention in schools which is due to them. They were received as latecomers; when they were taught, they occupied a place outside the regular curriculum and were taught as 'extras' or spare time activities. The right teachers were not easy to find; the rooms and equipment demanded have not always been available, and the subjects have, therefore, lacked a good tradition in the schools. (pp. 122–3)

> There is, however, another reason for their neglect. When they were adopted into the curriculum they occupied an uneasy position, lying apart from the rest of it; there seemed uncertainty – less perhaps as regards art – how they were related to other subjects, and they themselves did not always justify their inclusion on grounds which carried conviction . . . (p. 123)

> We submit . . . that . . . they [these subjects] have been hampered in finding their right place, partly by their late claim to a place in the regular curriculum, partly by inadequate presentation and appreciation of their case, and from these causes certain disabilities have resulted. (p. 124)

As disabilities Norwood listed:

a   Hesitation on the part of some heads, faced with shortage of space and equipment and an already overcrowded curriculum, to support the development of subjects which offered so little in terms of 'results'

b   Shortage of well-qualified and gifted teachers

c   Tendency among smaller schools to depend upon part-timers

d   Inadequate premises and shortage of equipment

e   Pressure put upon arts teachers to make their subjects examinable and so justifiable. (Norwood was bitterly opposed to this idea.)

Newsom, twenty years later,* complained that music tended to disappear from the curriculum of the 'more able' pupils at the end of the third year of secondary schooling. It is our experience that all arts subjects tend to disappear at that stage from the curriculum for most pupils. The particular 'disability' that Newsom

* Central Advisory Council for Education (England), *Half our Future* [The Newsom Report] (HMSO, 1963).

anticipated was that young school-leavers would come to consider the arts as 'neither useful nor prestige' subjects. Schools Council *Enquiry 1: Young School Leavers* (HMSO, 1968) substantiates Newsom's findings.

The arts in secondary schools are still beset by the same problems: inadequate resources, poor accommodation, shortage of good teachers, rigid timetabling, overloaded classes and a thoroughly depressed status. Our own initial survey of arts teachers in thirty-six schools disclosed that almost half the teachers were dissatisfied with their equipment and more than half with the premises in which they worked. Drama and music were the least well provided for among the arts subjects. In an unpublished HMI report on art in Devon secondary schools 1967 to 1969 reference is made to DES Building Bulletin No. 34, *Secondary School Design*, followed by this remark:

> Allocation of space for art in new buildings – usually one multi-purpose room – compares unfavourably with that provided for other subjects . . . (Not, we suggest, with that provided for other *arts* subjects.) Premises in general fall short of requirements in accommodation and equipment so far as present needs are concerned.

The education of the finer feelings

The most striking failure had not been what Norwood called the failure of 'presentation'. It was certainly true that the arts had failed either to make or substantiate their case. But, as a reading of the reports themselves makes only too clear, the traditional claims made for the arts in education were fundamentally flawed – the failure was at the conceptual rather than at the presentational level. Although drawing had been introduced into the school curriculum in the second half of the nineteenth century for mainly practical reasons, the tendency since then had been to see the arts as having not so much a practical as a cultural purpose. The assumption is everywhere implicit in the reports we have just been discussing that the significance of the arts lies in their contribution to a 'well-rounded education' – and this has a very different connotation from what we would mean by 'a balanced curriculum'. They are speaking of the cultivation of finer feelings. Arts education has been traditionally expected to effect a gradual improvement in the level of public taste, to lay the foundations for healthy and worth-while leisure-time pursuits and, by affording emotional release and creative satisfaction, to contribute to the personal development of tomorrow's artisans and professional citizens.

The attribution of quasi-magical properties to the arts in education is probably still more widespread than might be supposed. It surely forms part of whatever

29

rationale lies behind the assumption that arts teachers are somehow or another committed to the preservation of what is called 'our cultural heritage', and to the exposure of the young to its beneficent influence. In 1965 a White Paper on the arts* offered this point of view:

> Today a searching reappraisal of the whole situation in relation to cultural standards and opportunities is in progress. More and more people begin to appreciate that the exclusion of so many for so long from the best of our cultural heritage [referred to elsewhere as 'the best in music, painting, sculpture and literature'] can become as damaging to the privileged minority as to the underprivileged majority.

The popular idea of the role of the arts in school today has a long tradition and is directly linked to this limited notion of art itself. It is as divorced from the living culture of the people as it is from the world of the serious contemporary artist. Arts education is still generally understood outside the arts departments to be concerned with the transmission and exploitation of 'the best of our cultural heritage' on the assumption that the extension of cultural privilege will exert a powerful civilizing influence on young people. Indirectly, somehow or other, arts education *might* help to make a better Britain too.† It is this conception that most seriously circumscribes the prospects for arts teaching in the schools because it largely defines and determines their status.

a In the first place the arts are pegged down firmly among hobbies, worthy pastimes and leisure activities generally.

b Most young people feel that the leisure activities of the middle aged and the middle class are no concern of theirs. They have their own tastes in music, reading, clothes, films and television programmes – and these pursuits come well down their list of priorities anyway.

---

* *A Policy for the Arts: the First Steps* (HMSO, 1965).

† Lord Goodman, chairman of the Arts Council said in a House of Lords debate in 1967:

> I believe that there is a crucial state in the country at this moment. I believe that young people lack values, lack certainties, lack guidance; that they need something to turn to; and need it more desperately than they have needed it at any time in our history – certainly, at any time which I can recollect. I do not say that the Arts will furnish a total solution, but I believe that . . . once young people are captured for the Arts they are redeemed from many of the dangers which confront them at the moment and which have been occupying the attention of the Government in a completely unprofitable and destructive fashion. I believe that here we have constructive work to do which can be of inestimable value. (*Hansard, House of Lords*, 19 April 1967, c. 246)

The relevance of arts education

When one considers the evidence of the Schools Council's *Enquiry 1: Young School Leavers* (HMSO, 1968), whatever reservations one might have concerning the suggested priorities of the pupils and the alleged gap between them and those of the teachers – and we shall come back to that point – it is clear that arts education does not commend itself particularly to parents. The real issues are unmistakable and are, if anything, becoming increasingly urgent: the boys must get good jobs and the girls, if not jobs, then husbands. Schools cease to be worth taking seriously outside the context of these basic issues – apart from providing for a basic physical and moral fitness. While many parents, in our experience, were ready to take an interest in their children's arts activities, few would go so far as to say that the arts were essential to the serious purposes of secondary education, and strong opposition was aroused by any suggestion of an artistic career for their own child. That the schools, whatever teachers might say they feel as individuals, largely endorse the attitude of the parents, is beyond question. It would seem that many schools are well aware of their strengths and would not wish, even if they were able, to adjust to a different set of priorities.

Using its own criteria, the survey points out that the schools do not have a very good record in the field of 'affective education'. In the sample of young school-leavers it is pointed out that,

> apart from mathematics and English the subjects most widely valued were the practical vocational and practical domestic ones. These were very generally also found to be interesting. Of the subjects which might be expected to be enjoyed in themselves or valued because they widened interests, namely art, handicrafts, music, physical education and games, only physical education and games were to any extent found interesting or seen as useful . . . The implication is that schools are on the whole much more successful in their instrumental role, that is in providing knowledge and skills which are useful, than in giving young people satisfying means of expressing their emotions and using their energies. (p. 70, para. 123)

It is perhaps revealing that such an indictment should have caused so little apparent concern. One factor in their instrumental success is of course the deployment by the schools of time and money to that end.

We analysed the balance of curriculum provision in secondary modern, comprehensive and grammar schools (years 1–5) in a DES national sample.* Tables

* Most of the following data are taken from DES, *Statistics of Education*, Special Series No. 1: Survey of the Curriculum and Deployment of Teachers (Secondary Schools), 1965–66, Part 1: Teachers (HMSO, 1968).

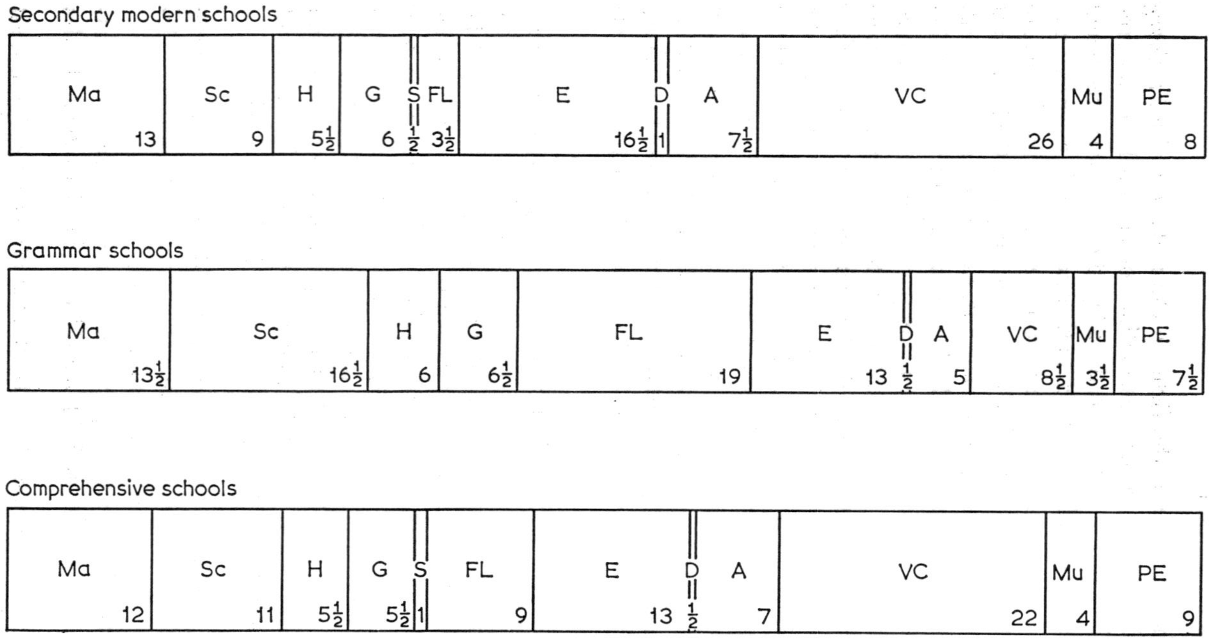

Secondary modern schools

Ma	Sc	H	G	S	FL	E	D	A	VC	Mu	PE
13	9	5½	6	½	3½	16½	1	7½	26	4	8

Grammar schools

Ma	Sc	H	G	FL	E	D	A	VC	Mu	PE
13½	11	16½	6½	19	13½	1½	5	8½	3½	7½

Comprehensive schools

Ma	Sc	H	G	S	FL	E	D	A	VC	Mu	PE
12	11	5½	5½	1	9	13½	1½	7	22	4	9

Key Ma = Mathematics   S = Social studies   D = Drama
     Sc = Science   FL = Foreign languages   A = Art
     H = History   E = English   Mu = Music
     G = Geography   VC = Vocational and domestic crafts   PE = Physical education

Fig. 2 Actual curriculum provision in secondary modern, grammar and comprehensive schools – taken from DES national sample (1st–5th years – in percentages).

1–3 and Figures 2–4 show the provision of time for particular subjects as a percentage of the total curriculum. In the case of all three types of school the arts will be seen at a considerable disadvantage in comparison with the academic–vocational bloc. It will also be noticed that the basic weighting given to the 'instrumental' subjects, as opposed to the others, is strikingly similar for all schools (see Fig. 2).

The arts subjects (excluding English, and dance when it is part of the PE curriculum) occupy about 10 per cent of tuition time in secondary schools – and this is more or less the same for all types of school. Science subjects (which include mathematics in the DES statistics), and languages (including English) all occupy about twice as much tuition time in secondary modern and comprehensive schools, and three-and-a-half times as much in grammar and non-maintained schools (see Table 1).

Table 1 Tuition time provided in different subjects (in percentages)

Subject	Non-maintained	Grammar	Compre-hensive	Secondary modern	All schools
General studies	6·0	7·0	11·0	10·5	9·0
Technology and handicraft	1·0	4·0	9·0	10·0	8·0
Agricultural and rural studies	0·1	—	0·6	1·5	1·0
Science (including mathematics)	31·0	31·0	23·0	21·0	24·0
Geographical, social, business studies	7·0	7·0	9·0	8·0	8·0
Home economics	2·0	4·0	7·0	11·0	8·0
Languages/Literature (including English)	32·0	30·0	21·0	18·0	22·0
Arts other than languages	11·0	10·0	9·0	10·0	10·0
Music, drama and visual arts	9·0	8·0	11·0	11·0	10·0
TOTALS	100·0	100·0	100·0	100·0	100·0

(numbers have been rounded)

Changes in the patterns of tuition time are discernible as pupils progress through the school: the arts declining from 12 per cent to 7 per cent of all tuition time; language teaching (including English) remaining fairly constant, but at different levels according to the type of school; more science being taught in sixth forms than lower down the school (see Table 2).

Table 2 Tuition time given to arts subjects, compared with other subjects, over secondary-school period (in percentages)

Type of school	Science	Languages/Literature	Arts
Secondary modern			
1st–3rd years	20	19	13
4th–5th years	21	16	9
6th–8th years	26	21	7
Grammar			
1st–3rd years	27	31	10
4th–5th years	31	30	7
6th–8th years	36	28	7
Comprehensive			
1st–3rd years	21	22	12
4th–5th years	22	19	9
6th–8th years	32	23	7
Non-maintained schools			
1st–3rd years	25	33	13
4th–5th years	31	34	9
6th–8th years	36	30	6
All schools			
1st–3rd years	22	22	12
4th–5th years	25	21	9
6th–8th years	35	27	7

Arts = Music, drama and visual arts   Science = Biology, chemistry, physics, general science, mathematics   Languages/Literature = English, French, German, Greek, Latin, and other languages + literature

Simply in terms of numbers, there are two science or language teachers in our secondary schools to every one teacher involved in the arts (i.e. music, drama and the visual arts) and one significant if crude indication of the space occupied by a

34

subject in the school curriculum is the number of teachers involved in teaching it. Fifteen per cent of all secondary-school teachers have studied arts subjects: the picture varies according to the type of secondary school with the arts teacher, perhaps rather surprisingly, most in evidence in the secondary modern schools where it is difficult to see the arts acting as anything more significant than 'packing'. In the grammar school, arts teachers are usually outnumbered by about 3 to 1 when compared with either their science or language colleagues (see Fig. 3).

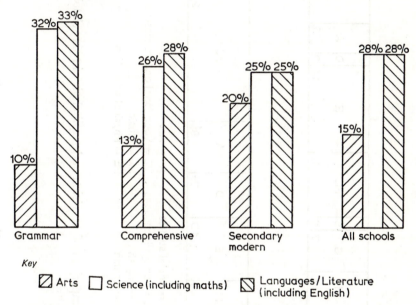

Fig. 3 Proportions of arts teachers in different types of secondary school.

In our research schools we asked the pupils to construct their own curriculum* and we then compared pupil choice with actual provision. In Figure 4 it is clearly shown that the pupils wished to reduce curriculum distortion significantly. Teachers in the schools, given much the same task, left the balance of the curriculum virtually intact.

Actual provision in our research schools amounted to a curriculum weighting of 4:1 against the arts and PE. The pupils would have wished to reduce this to

* For details see Robert Witkin's *The Intelligence of Feeling* (Heinemann Educational, 1974), pp. 139–68.

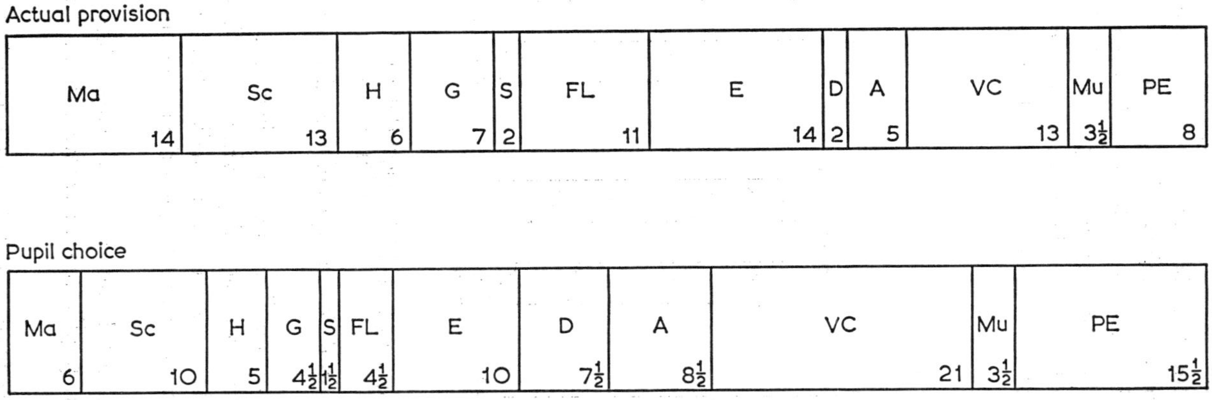

Actual provision

Ma	Sc	H	G	S	FL	E	D	A	VC	Mu	PE
14	13	6	7	2	11	14	2	5	13	$3\frac{1}{2}$	8

Pupil choice

Ma	Sc	H	G	S	FL	E	D	A	VC	Mu	PE
6	10	5	$4\frac{1}{2}$	$1\frac{1}{2}$	$4\frac{1}{2}$	10	$7\frac{1}{2}$	$8\frac{1}{2}$	21	$3\frac{1}{2}$	$15\frac{1}{2}$

Key Ma = Mathematics   S = Social studies   A = Art
     Sc = Science   FL = Foreign languages   VC = Vocational and domestic crafts
     H = History   E = English   Mu = Music
     G = Geography   D = Drama   PE = Physical education

Fig. 4 The curriculum: a comparison of provision and pupil choice in six schools (1st–5th years – in percentages).

nearer 2:1. (See Table 3.) Their rather more drastic revisions, however, amounted to a severe cutback of the academic curriculum (of mathematics and language teaching especially) and a huge demand for increased participatory and expressive opportunities, through the vocational crafts, the arts, PE and games. Our empirical research entirely supported my initial impression of the basic frustration of many secondary-school pupils.

Table 3   Summary of actual curriculum provision and pupil choice of curriculum (in percentages)

Curriculum	Actual provision	Pupil choice
Academic	68	42
Non-academic	32	55
Academic–vocational	80	63
Other	20	34

The barrenness of the secondary-school curriculum is the result of an undeclared conspiracy between society and the schools, and the victims are the children. In the face of such a conspiracy no amount of official exhortation or administrative and organizational shuffling has had or ever could have the slightest effect. We have to look for other means of reform.

I have been suggesting that, although their cause has not lacked its apologists, the arts have always been dogged by misunderstanding and misconception as far as their educational function has been concerned. Before moving on to look at the situation from the arts teacher's point of view it is worth noting that, whereas it would be true to say that most people have remained unimpressed by the arts' case, popular disregard of the arts in school arises not only from a sense of their irrelevance but also from a strong suspicion that they are actually dangerous: socially disruptive and morally ambivalent. One headmaster expressed the situation this way:

You can't be 'obscene' in science, and therefore those who are worried about pornography and obscenity might take refuge in mathematical calculation, and coldness would be a certain way of insulating oneself from possible intrusions. Moaning Johnnies and Jillies complain about the state of the nation and the way things are going to the dogs: these are often equated with those who take part in things like dancing and pop music and unexplainable art and this is all seen to be a deterioration of morale or moral fibre or something like this . . .

It is not uncommon to find prejudice of this vague but virulent kind in many staff common-rooms.

Arts teachers are different

The arts are subjects apart and arts teachers tend to be teachers apart. This is of course an inevitable consequence of the standing of the subjects they teach – but, as we discovered from our study of the DES statistics, there are other factors related to their professional training, careers and actual deployment in the schools that tend to set arts teachers apart from their colleagues and at some disadvantage.

Their training tends to be more specialized and less 'academic' than that of their colleagues. This has perhaps some advantages – the arts subjects attract more specialists than the sciences or languages (only 10 per cent of arts teaching is done by non-specialists, 18 per cent of science, 20 per cent of language), but it might be argued that there are fewer alternative modes of employment open to them. But the fact that the special training of graduate arts teachers is carried on very often in institutions devoted exclusively to the arts, and not in multi-discipline universities, endorses the sense of mystique associated with the arts. It also makes for quite a complex network of routes or avenues of recruitment (see Fig. 5).

Teachers of the arts have had some nine choices* open to them – though some of these are likely to be closed in the near future. Seventy-one replies to our

* 1. Degree (university or CNAA).
2. Degree followed by Postgraduate Certificate of Education taken at a university department or a college of education.
3. Degree equivalent (college of art, college of music).
4. Degree equivalent followed by PGCE course (as above), or its equivalent (for example, ATD/ATC at college of art).
5. Diploma, certificate (college of art, college of music).
6. Diploma, certificate, followed by a professional course at a college of education.
7. Specialist Teacher's Certificates (course at specialist college followed by course at college of education).
8. Teacher's Certificate (college of education).
9. B Ed degree (college of education).

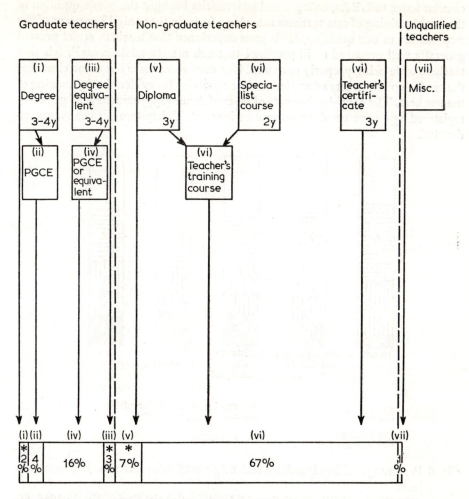

Figure content (boxes and percentages):

Graduate teachers | Non-graduate teachers | Unqualified teachers

(i) Degree 3–4y → (ii) PGCE

(iii) Degree equivalent 3–4y → (iv) PGCE or equivalent

(v) Diploma 3y → (vi) Teacher's training course

(vi) Specialist course 2y → (vi) Teacher's training course

(vi) Teacher's certificate 3y

(vii) Misc.

(i)(ii) *2% 4% | (iv) 16% | (iii) *3% (v) *7% | (vi) 67% | (vii) %

* Qualified teachers with no professional training. These avenues were closed from January 1974 (see DES Circular 18/69).

Fig. 5 Secondary-school arts teachers – avenues of recruitment.
(Data from DES, *Statistics of Education*, Special Series No. 1: 1965–66, Part 1: Teachers. The DES survey was taken prior to B Ed output. This is now a widening avenue of recruitment.)

39

circular letter to LEAs, colleges and universities brought the whole question of the initial training of arts teachers into sharp focus in that only 13 per cent of the respondents to our question, 'Is it your experience that teachers are at present generally well prepared or ill prepared to teach arts to adolescents?', felt that teachers were being properly prepared. Our correspondence has made clear that the confusion felt in arts education in the schools is also evident in the training of the teachers. The considerable vote of no confidence (approximately 55 per cent) registered by our respondents cannot be ignored. Thirty-two per cent were undecided.

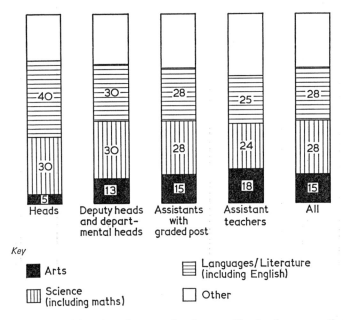

Fig. 6 Percentage of headteachers and other staff who have studied arts subjects.
(Data from DES, *Statistics of Education*, Special Series No. 1: 1965–66, Part 1: Teachers.)

It has for a long while been recognized that graduate status is an important feature in a teacher's general professional viability and we are now rapidly moving towards a time when we may expect teaching to be an all-graduate profession. There can be little question that graduate status has a considerable bearing on career prospects. If we look at the incidence of arts, science and language trained teachers at the various levels of responsibility in the schools (Fig. 6) we

40

find that arts teachers are rather overrepresented at the assistant teacher level and dramatically underrepresented as headteachers. We find* that, although arts teachers are 15 per cent of all teachers, only 5 per cent of all headteachers have studied arts subjects. Science teachers are fairly represented at both levels; on the other hand, a much higher proportion of headteachers have studied languages and literature than would be expected on statistical grounds.

To attempt an explanation would be pure speculation, although the high proportion of non-graduates among arts teachers must play some part. Whatever the cause, the situation is likely to affect the emphasis on arts in the curriculum, the self-concept of arts teachers and the status of the arts teacher in the eyes of his colleagues.

The lot of the arts teacher is made more unfortunate in that 80 per cent of arts graduates have qualifications which have been recognized, not as straightforward degrees but as of degree equivalence: for example, they have an award from a college or department of art and design, or a graduate diploma from a college of music. And there is something, not necessarily inferior, but basically different about having degree equivalent status.

However this is of little concern to most full-time teachers of the arts, as 75 per cent of them tend to be non-graduate in any case. This is a significantly higher proportion than obtains among secondary teachers as a whole of whom only 43 per cent are non-graduates. (The figure for science teachers is 57 per cent and for language teachers 45 per cent.) Arts teachers will not feel this distinction in secondary modern schools, where most other teachers are also non-graduates. However, in grammar, comprehensive and non-maintained schools the arts are likely to have fewer graduate staff than other departments and this could make a decisive difference in status. No suggestion that quality of teaching is in any way related to graduate status is of course implied. We are concerned here simply with the delicate question of intra-professional esteem and with the extent to which arts teachers might well feel themselves to be – and are indeed seen by their colleagues to be – of less than equal standing when conflicts over rival claims to time and resources develop.

The arts lack vital bargaining power. To what has been said so far add that the arts subjects have to rely more than other subjects upon assistance from part-time staff – 10 per cent of all arts teachers are part-timers against 5 per cent of language and 3 per cent of science teachers – and we have a strong argument in support of our contention that the arts subjects are largely in the hands of a group of men and women whose professional standing and involvement is felt

* DES, *Statistics of Education*, Special Series No. 1: 1965–66, Part 1: Teachers.

adviser acts not just as an expert and as a manager of local resources, but also as both an important link, capable of drawing his teachers together into a dynamic relationship, and as a vital channel of inspiration and new thinking. There can be little doubt of the serious disadvantage to any school system lacking the assistance of such a full-time expert. More important perhaps was the finding that 60 per cent of the teachers investigated had to work outside the timetable in order to complete what they would regard as their normal teaching programme, and that over 80 per cent were involved in running extracurricular activities on a voluntary basis after school. Arts teachers may be more or less hard pressed than their non-arts colleagues: clearly they are working under some strain, and if they have little time or energy left for in-service courses or for their own painting it is perhaps scarcely their fault.

The extent of arts teachers' involvement in the world of art is not easy to assess but the impression we have is that the teacher who practises his art is not as common as one might expect – indeed few teachers are able to find the time to keep abreast of current developments in their own field. As one art teacher frankly confessed to us:

> I need charging up at times and sometimes I think, right, there are a couple of exhibitions up in London I ought to go to but I just haven't got the time or the stamina to get up there and back and be able to feed it back into my job. There are times when I feel I ought to go and do a year in an art college – to start all over again – because the time's getting on, but my husband teaches evening classes and now we have a baby, and well . . .

Contact with the contemporary arts, or with the living world of the art of the past would seem to be an indispensable source of personal stimulus and nourishment. A teacher's personal involvement in the processes of art is likely to give his teaching relevance and vitality – arts teaching will become neither perfunctory nor mechanical in his hands. Like any other system – organic, electronic or social – an arts department without effective and vital links with its environment will suffer progressive breakdown. Our study of the extent to which teachers are able to establish and sustain links with stimulating and revitalizing elements beyond the classroom, both professional and artistic, emphatically reinforces an impression of serious personal isolation. Contacts outside the school are vital to him.

The arts teacher's isolation, both as an individual and as a member of a professional group apart, emerges strongly from our inquiries and supplementary studies. It is at the same time a cause and a factor of the peripheral role of the arts. However, it would miss the point entirely to suppose that the situation could be improved simply by rationalizing his training or upgrading his qualifi-

44

cations – or merely by integrating the different arts subjects into a single organizational unit. It is infinitely more important that each arts teacher should establish his control of the arts curriculum. That has to be the means of reform mentioned earlier.

Summary

Generally, for all practical purposes, arts education remains a matter of only peripheral concern. Neither the arts subjects nor the teachers have ever been taken seriously. Such has been the reluctant conclusion of every major educational report published in the last fifty years, and such is ours. We have cited a number of factors in explanation and have described some of the consequences. Most damaging to the cause of arts education has been the persistent lack of a serviceable theoretical foundation that would lend it authority and guide its development.

Young people are manifestly bored with the traditional secondary-school curriculum and some of them ask whether this must necessarily be so: 'We should have more say in what we do, some of our lessons are very boring, and for fourth-year girls *this is not right*.'

That the pupils in our research schools could ask so emphatically for more drama and more art must be a sign that arts teachers are now achieving some success in conditions that have often hitherto effectively emasculated their work. In the next chapter we shall look more particularly at recent developments within the arts curriculum. The impression is of considerable enthusiasm and energy. Unfortunately, despite the particular successes of gifted individuals, arts education has so far failed, through lack of focus and direction, to take advantage of the opportunities available in the present educational climate.

III. The arts curriculum and the intelligence of feeling

The disappointing performance of the arts in secondary schools referred to in the preceding chapter arises not simply from the constraints imposed upon arts teachers by the insignificant position traditionally accorded their subjects in the curriculum as a whole (English being the notable exception), but also from the confusion and contradiction to be found in the purposes and practice of many arts departments today. In *The Intelligence of Feeling* Robert Witkin uses a particular framework of his own for analysing in detail the arts curriculum of each of our six research schools. He probes the consciousness of the teachers concerned with respect to the subjects they teach, working his ideas through what he defines as their 'praxis'. In the brief review presented here my perspective is different: I take a more general view of the characteristic features of each of the arts subjects in order to highlight the major conflicts which divide arts teachers and which, in my opinion, effectively keep them in unproductive isolation.

English

English, as the cornerstone of the modern secondary-school curriculum, cannot of course rival the classics in educational pedigree; however, its present eminence is undisputed. The English teacher's authority rests on his claim on two of the three Rs of a general education. Parents, pupils and colleagues alike endorse his efforts in the teaching of reading and writing – and, should any of his charges be judged lacking in either of these skills, the responsibility is quickly laid at his door. All other teachers of the creative arts in school have some cause to envy him his unassailable position. His work is respected and its importance reflected in the size of his department and his generous allowance of timetable space. Among his fellow arts teachers he alone can claim to offer something that everybody wants. In recent years various research studies have drawn attention to the importance of the spoken as well as the written word. The key role of language acquisition in the mental, social and emotional growth of young children is now widely accepted, and English teachers are being asked to devise and test new methods of developing language skills both within and outside the school setting. The once rather academic study of linguistics is now arousing considerable general interest. All these fresh influences pointing to the critical role of language in education – together with the considerable efforts now being directed towards helping the new immigrant families – have, while adding to his responsibilities, served to confirm the crucial importance of the English teacher at all levels of education today.

Why has English been grouped in this report for study among the creative arts subjects? Many English teachers have little time for what has become known as 'creative' English. Certainly the English teacher is concerned to develop language skills, but to what extent is he seriously concerned with language as a medium of self-expression? To our considerable disappointment we found little evidence that such new approaches to English teaching as have long been canvassed by the National Association for the Teaching of English are making anything other than very slow progress. In our research schools English was given an unmistakably non-arts, non-creative, 'academic' profile by the pupils. In *Enquiry 1* the headteachers, and not the young school-leavers, set great store by poetry. Here is an excerpt from Robert Witkin's account of English teaching in the project's school sample:

> In effect some 70 per cent of the lessons were strongly 'academic' in their structure, concerned either with English language or more usually with working from the text of a play or poem in a strongly teacher-directed way. Some of this work was tied directly to an examination syllabus . . . only about 8 per cent of the lessons observed were devoted to any kind of creative writing exercise.

Considering the number of eminent and persuasive apologists that the creative writing movement has had over the years, it is sad to find the subject still so bogged down in tedious hack and journey work. The teaching of English literature – which, despite the much maligned examination boards, should provide scope for some arousal of and engagement with the pupil's feelings – is often a dreary labour with little encouragement to the pupil to offer his own necessarily immature responses. Books belong to the world of objects and pupils are trained in the public language of their appraisal. The dangers of encouraging self-expression among pupils are not inconsiderable – good men have been suspended for less.

Thus, on reflection, the lot of the English teacher may not be as enviable as the prestige of his position would suggest. His can be a cruel dilemma: usually intensely interested in literature himself and firmly committed, in spirit at least, to the notion that an individual's language should reflect and extend his personality, he frequently has to lower his sights and 'make do' with his O-level improbables and the writing of formal letters with the RoSLA group. Shades of

47

the prison house will darken the journals and poems and short stories of his young creative writers by the time they come to the end of their third year in secondary school. And he will be in no position to say why this should not be so.

Art

In an account of the history of art education in America, Elliot Eisner* gives a succinct analysis of the extent to which goals and practices have shifted over the years. Art was taught in the mid-nineteenth century 'because it was thought to develop the penmanship skills of the general school population'. Instruction was unsystematic and was justified 'in the name of cultural refinement'. Since then, arts education has acquired a number of new emphases without entirely losing any on the way. During the 1870s economic pressures pressed art education into the service of industry to produce skilled hands for the emerging textile and hardware industries. However, in the 1880s 'The growing concern with the child and his development . . . effected a shift towards the use of art for the ends of self-expression and self-realization'. By the late 1920s the influence of Freud in progressive education was strongly marked, and the prime concerns of art education became 'creativity and mental health'. This bias led naturally in the late 1940s and the 1950s to stress being laid upon 'process' rather than 'product'. Eisner concludes by detecting as the latest theme of art education 'a concern for the development of . . . the critical as well as the productive skills of the general student in art'.

David Manzella, in his *Educationists and the Evisceration of the Visual Arts* (International Textbook, 1963), argues vigorously for the reintroduction of the values of fine art into art education, complaining that the current underlying philosophy of art education 'emasculates art and allows it to become a meaningless diddle'. He goes on to say that the kernel of his thinking is that the teaching of art in general education should be directed towards aesthetic growth, through learning about art implemented by, but not centred on, studio experiences. Along with the teaching of art as a subject, there should be studio classes taught by competent creative and exhibiting artists available on an after-school, evening, and Saturday basis. The strength of the programme would reside in its promise of (i) literacy in the arts for all youngsters, and (ii) competent instruction and real challenges in the practice of art for the interested.

Sjoerd Hannema, in his *Fads, Fakes and Fantasies* (Macdonald, 1970), having mounted an attack on the current situation particularly in art colleges, makes a plea for a more 'professional' approach:

* 'Art education' in *Encyclopedia of Educational Research* (Collier-Macmillan, 4th edn, 1969), pp. 76–86.

What we need is a return to aesthetic criteria, to sound craftmanship, to a sense of pleasure in visual creation. Only the professional artist will be able to guide the amateur . . .

English teachers of art will probably recognize features of the American pattern in their own experience of the development of art education; however, some divergence of emphasis in recent years must be noted. Whereas the pressure to tighten up and defend the arts curriculum has led American educators to revise the notion of arts education as concerned fundamentally with the appreciation of works of art, in this country the same pressure has sent our teachers in quite another direction – towards what has come to be known as 'design education'. Our own special study of art teaching* sees the present situation in this country thus:

> The two extremes of the two main movements, towards design education or towards the expressive arts represent two very opposing points of view as to their educational function. Much of design education is concerned with analysis, research and the application of logic in problem-solving situations – with the cognitive aspects of education. Much emphasis in the expressive arts may be placed upon the role of feeling, intuition and personal expression – with the affective aspects of education. The ideological conflict (as to which way to go!) is not unlike that in France after the revolution, with the Classicists and the Romantics doing battle for official recognition as the artists of the revolution.

> The ideological stimulus for the design movement has stemmed mainly from Cardiff, Hornsey and the Schools Council Design and Craft Education Project at Keele University.† The movement towards expressive art has a longer history and more sources: Charity James' work at Goldsmith's Curriculum Laboratory to visual/aural education courses at Hornsey and the development of the integrated day pattern of teaching in the primary schools have all been influential factors.

Of all the subjects with which this study has been concerned, except for English, art has probably the most secure place in the general curriculum, art teachers having a sense of tradition and of their subject's continuing development to sustain them. Yet, at present, art education at all levels in this country is in some disarray, a prey to individual quirks and preoccupations. The 1971 Department of Education and Science Education Survey 11, *Art in Schools*, speaks

* Published as R. Clement, *Art for Whose Sake?*, Themes in Education series (Exeter Institute of Education, 1972).
† Books for teachers and pupils, and filmstrips, from this project are published for the Council by Edward Arnold (1974–75).

of the 'extremely uneven and complicated pattern' of art education at secondary level. As Robert Clement, the writer of our special study, points out, there has in recent years been a noticeable failure of initiative and momentum in art teaching:

> There has not been anything like the radical re-thinking about the actual system of teaching amongst art teachers that we have seen in maths and drama and language teaching over the last decade. Where new systems have been introduced or tried they have been largely image- or style-producing systems, which have affected the appearance of what is being produced in the art rooms but rarely the pattern or method of teaching.

This sense of inertia is evident also in the syllabuses of the various schools examinations boards. Clement suggests that 'the content (or skill/area requirements) of the English art examinations has changed very little over the last twenty years'. He continues:

> One or two anachronisms have disappeared (e.g. JMB paper in decoration of given flat shapes) and non-figurative work has been provided for by some boards since the mid-sixties (fifty years after the first pure abstract painting was produced) – but, despite minor variations, the actual content has not reflected the major changes that have taken place in professional art practice or even taken much account of fundamental changes in attitude as to the educational function of art teaching during the last two decades.

David Manzella speaks for many art educators on both sides of the Atlantic when he says,

> The future meaningfulness of the visual arts within general education is dependent on the establishment of a more reasonable philosophic base for the field and its generous support and implementation.

Others see the problem in slightly different terms: art education has to have some manifest purpose, and must be demonstrably useful. Teachers have grown uneasy over the subjugation of craftsmanship to the rather nebulous demand for 'creativity', itself an educational concept of barely ten years' standing, as yet scarcely understood. It is easier to argue and substantiate the case for the 'usefulness' of courses in art appreciation or design education or visual literacy, rather than for the usefulness of providing opportunities for children to 'express' themselves.

The truth of the situation, as far as the adolescent is concerned, is described by Dick Field in *Change in Art Education* (Routledge & Kegan Paul, 1970):

> The arts are not strange or esoteric to the young child; he moves in them as naturally as a fish in water . . . But children grow up; and the forms taken

by their growing efforts to structure their experience are not always acceptable in terms of taste or social usage or morality. In the arts, as elsewhere, the child comes up against authority. He learns that some subjects are taboo, that there are prescribed forms, that there are techniques to be learned . . . But for most children by this stage things have gone irreparably wrong. Art has become ART – unattainable, remote; what he does himself is no longer functional in terms of his needs and interests; is merely a vestigial thing, a reminder of times past. The gap is too wide; and many children are left to assume that they will never be artists, that they are left on the outside.

Drama

The DES Education Survey 2, *Drama* (HMSO, 1967) betrays a similar dissatisfaction with inadequately considered 'creative' and 'expressive' approaches to work with young people.

> Improvisation lies at the heart of school drama. Its contribution to the growth of children can be considerable. But a great deal of improvisation is shapeless and without clear purpose. Its aims are in urgent need of clarification. Much of the uncertainty in improvisation lies in the widespread use of movement by teachers of drama without a clear idea of its nature. Too often it is thought to be 'good for the children' and to help their 'self-expression'. Much movement is done to music which is often mishandled so that it provides little in the way of musical, physical, or dramatic experience. (p. 107)

The dilemma of drama educators seems to be to resolve the rival claims of 'theatre studies' and 'participation'. The survey recommends, for older pupils, a firm orientation towards the study of plays 'for their own sake' – on which, it is felt, too little time is currently spent. This implies the development of existing links with English, with the implication firmly underlined that:

> If we admit that the activities we have described as drama have any educational significance, can we deny that they are also the beginning of the process that ends in Aeschylus, Shakespeare, Ibsen? (p. 110)

For 'both halves of our future'? Drama teachers can be forgiven surely for feeling that this line of argument offers no through road to relevance, engagement and respectability but, once again, an educational *cul-de-sac*.

While agreeing with the view that the aims not only of drama but of all the arts in education 'are in urgent need of clarification', and sharing the widespread uneasiness over the uncritical and self-indulgent nature of much arts teaching, we can neither accept that arts education should become predominantly another

51

problem-solving activity in the cognitive field, nor that its future lies in helping more children come to terms with their 'cultural heritage'. The relevance of the arts in education is to the world of feeling and, although it has proved difficult to develop an effective theory of arts education on that premise, it is our conviction that nothing less will serve.

The world of the drama teacher is as fraught with confusion as that of his colleague in the art department, though he may feel encouraged by the considerable interest and activity generated in his field during the past decade. There remains a fundamental controversy over the role and purpose of drama in the schools. 'Drama in education' based on the survey just referred to begins:

> Educational drama has grown rapidly in recent years and is still expanding but there is as yet no clearly definable discipline that can be so identified. There is, for example, no general agreement on its relation to English with its literary and linguistic content, to movement, dance and music. Yet some clarification is needed to prevent the quantity of work outstripping its quality. (DES, *Reports on Education*, No. 50, November 1968)

The survey itself comes to no positive conclusion: 'We do not wish to make a final pronouncement as to whether drama is a subject or not' – a diffidence that teachers and advisers can hardly be expected to find either encouraging or helpful. The question which goes unanswered in this survey is not so much the one the authors draw attention to: 'What should be the aims of improvisation or more generally of drama in education?', but one that is altogether more fundamental: 'What is the essential and unique nature of the dramatic experience itself?' All the agonizing over the 'integrity of the subject' and its relationship to English or physical education points to this basic need for clarification of the exact nature of the experience we are offering children in drama. In the absence of an answer to our question all other issues tend to become trivial, and it proves impossible to try and think about inter-subject relationships.

Music

With music education we are yet again in difficulties over the lack of a basic consensus. Erwin Schneider, writing about music education in the United States in the 1969 *Encyclopedia of Educational Research*, reported:

> Little agreement appears to exist between persons holding different positions in education on the specific role and objectives of music education. For example, Jones (1961) and Kelley (1962) found little agreement on the

importance and function of music in the schools among superintendents, principals, and music teachers. Noah (1963), somewhat earlier, reported little evidence of a 'profound' statement of philosophy in the literature published by state departments of education. Freeman (1955) and Ernst (1955) found only a slight relationship between the program recommendations of the MENC [Music Educators National Conference] and practices in the schools they studied. The data from reports such as these suggest that a common philosophy of music education does not as yet exist in the schools.

Schneider goes on to look more closely at the teaching of what is frequently called 'general music', (classroom music available to all pupils) and finds that 'purposes and objectives . . . do not appear to have been standardized to any extent' and that 'some confusion exists about the real objectives of the activities and learnings in such classes'. Specific objectives for such classes often vary greatly. The most prominent musical activity in American schools is choral singing, supported in varying degrees by 'listening and study of musical fundamentals'. At the level of classroom practice there is thus a greater degree of uniformity in the teaching of music than in the teaching of the other arts subjects we have so far considered. This uniformity is not, however, the result of a common understanding among music teachers of the educational function of their subject, but is more probably an indication of a narrowness of outlook and a deeply-rooted inertia that long kept their subject free of the controversy over self-expression and creativity. So the music teacher today, while faced with considerable problems in terms of rendering his work meaningful to the majority of his students, does not share the same problems with teachers of art and drama. Music lags behind art and drama in several respects, and has remained largely aloof from the whole child-centred movement in education with all its ramifications. As Schneider points out, the classical objective of classroom music teaching has been 'the promotion of a better understanding and appreciation of *music*'.

Music faces possibly the sternest task of all the traditional arts subjects. Several factors can be offered in explanation: the alleged 'remoteness' of the traditional music curriculum from the lives of young people, the cultural and temporal gaps between teachers and taught, the inappropriateness of the music teachers' training, the demands on mind and skill that the reading of music and the mastery of a musical instrument present for many pupils. Perhaps, too, there is something inherent in the very immediacy of music itself, in its direct and explicit emotionalism that proves an obstacle for self-conscious adolescents in the formal school setting. It is certainly less easy and less 'natural' (or 'normal') for most western people to compose music than, say, to write, or even to paint. And music-making is rather less private than either of these other two activities. The disjunction between the growing complexity of an adolescent's emotional life and his capacity to command the means of adequate musical expression may ultimately prove too inhibiting without support of a very special kind from the music teacher. Perhaps music is, as many musicians have insisted to us, rather a special case after all.

Of course music has always meant an interpretative rather than a creative experience for most of us – we sing other men's songs, play other men's tunes. The creative use of sound as a medium of self-expression does not come easily: improvisation for example, a feature of much creative drama these days, is not generally an important aspect of the work in school and college music departments – and that is a pity. In recent years, creative music has received encouragement from the innovative work of musician–teachers such as Peter Aston, Brian Dennis, Terence Dwyer, George Self, Peter Maxwell-Davies, John Paynter and R. Murray Schafer. However, my own guess is that music teachers in schools generally are in desperate need of a clearer understanding of, and greater unanimity over, their educational function. Only from such an understanding and such unanimity of purpose can we expect a relevant and effective music curriculum to be developed.

Dance

The project's original brief included the study of dance, film and photography. We have been unable to carry out inquiries very far in these fields. These subjects are rarely taught by specialists as disciplines in their own right – for example, photography and mass media studies generally are still in an embryonic stage of development and, despite Newsom, remain, in our view, seriously neglected in the schools. In the colleges and departments of education media studies rarely rise above the level of a course in audio-visual aids. We were particularly disappointed by the apparent failure of dance to establish itself in secondary schools as anything more serious than a pleasant if sometimes embarrassing form of recreation for girls, and we asked Susan Morris, herself a teacher of dance, to investigate the situation for us. Mrs Morris received completed questionnaires from 347 secondary-school teachers of dance and thirty-one lecturers in dance in colleges of education. In her questionnaire Mrs Morris attempted to explore the aims of dance education, the problems experienced by dance teachers in their work, and their views on their training. The college questionnaires produced information that revealed some significant inconsistencies between departmental aims and the actual training programme or college dance curriculum.

From what the teachers had to say, Mrs Morris came to the conclusion that there is considerable confusion concerning the aims of dance education. In consequence, dance teachers are being inadequately prepared for their work and, once in the schools, are invariably recruited by the PE departments. It would seem that dance is as severely hindered by its dependence upon PE as drama used to be by virtue of its association with English. Many dance teachers, who are well aware of the creative and expressive potential of their subject, and happily recalling their own intensely personal experience at college, tend to feel very unsure of themselves when it comes to developing these aspects of their work with children and to fall back, with some reluctance, upon teaching skills that have some demonstrable, if limited, purpose and that can be fairly easily assessed.

As with the other arts subjects, dance education has its own internal factions. And, as with the other subjects, they arise at least in part from confusion at a conceptual level. In dance they tend to polarize about the twin features common to all the performing arts: execution or performance and composition or the creation of form. Crudely expressed, the controversy lies between those who see dance primarily as another means of physical development and of increasing physical skills, and those who feel that, by creating their own form in this particular medium, children can further their aesthetic and, more significantly, their emotional education. There is a school of opinion that would give priority to the training of the body, to the mastery of technique, and its methods are built around a complex system of exercises. An equally popular alternative approach stresses the arousal of personal feeling and its relatively free and unstructured expression in physical movement. Their differences may be more apparent than real, for few teachers would advocate technique for its own sake or would recommend for all children the kind of training that might be appropriate for the would-be professional dancer. Also, few would deny that expression and composition make increasing demands on individual skills. In suggesting that dance belongs firmly among the creative and expressive arts I would recommend its separation from PE, though this might only be necessary in the short term.

Mrs Morris concludes her report with some stiff comment directed at the colleges:

> There is a clear need for a more rigorous investigation of dance education than I have been able to undertake and also for some definite reappraisal of the lead and direction given by the colleges. At present they are not producing the right calibre of teacher and dance is thus failing to attain the position it deserves in the schools' curriculum.

Here again, then, we are thrown back upon basic issues: 'Why dance education?' and 'What kind of teachers for what kind of a curriculum?' The whole point and purpose of dance education has to be more clearly established if it is to move out of no-man's-land. My own feeling is that, like music, dance is potentially at least as rich in education experience as art and drama, and it is in the fields of music and dance that I would hope to see the greatest advances in arts education made in the next ten years.

The Intelligence of Feeling

Each of the arts subjects faces its own particular set of problems at the present time; each provides evidence of confusion, even conflict, over its function in a programme of general secondary education. Different emphases within the arts curriculum as a whole seem to polarize thus. On the one hand, under pressure to establish themselves within an essentially product-oriented, instrumental, externally validated milieu, arts teachers are seeking a functional, utilitarian role. English, as we have seen, has always had this character. Art teachers seek to promote visual literacy and regroup as design departments; drama teachers, through role play, 'gaming' and the documentary, feel that they are developing social skills, social consciousness – not to say a social conscience; dance, in the shadow of P E, is measured against criteria of physical and psychological growth; music usually finds its function in school life either in its ritualistic capacity (celebrating the school's identity through religious or secular ceremonial) or in terms of the conservation of what is called our cultural heritage. Arts teachers who favour performances, critical appreciation, exhibitions and art history frequently do so in order to give their teaching a clear, definable and to some extent assessable purpose. Even so-called 'creative' work, as Robert Witkin points out in the central section of his book, can suffer radical distortion in the interests of this kind of functionalism.

Opposed to this position are those (often the same) teachers who remain convinced that the arts have a unique role in education, clearly distinguishable from – yet complementary to – the mediated, externally-determined curriculum of the 'Right'. They are the teachers of the 'Left' – see J. S. Bruner's *On Knowing: Essays for the Left Hand* (Harvard University Press, 1962). They insist upon the personal and expressive impulse of art. Self-realization through creative art is their goal. However, their case has never been adequately substantiated, and their curriculum is disparagingly regarded as 'cack-handed'. The conflict I have been describing is resolved, more often than not, on the grounds of expediency rather than educational merit. For many arts teachers theirs has become an intolerable situation.

The Intelligence of Feeling is the project's response to the predicament of arts education depicted in this report. It is our view that the prime concern of the arts curriculum should be with the emotional development of the child through

56

creative self-expression – Robert Witkin's 'subject–reflexive action'. He makes the point thus:

> The creative arts provide instances of highly developed uses of subject–reflexive action. They stand in relation to the intelligence of feeling as the sciences do to logical reasoning. The failure to develop arts curricula in schools systematically and to give a priority to subject–reflexive action and its development which is in line with its vital importance in the adaptive process, will almost certainly have to be overcome if schools are to meet the adaptational requirements of the future. (p. 30)

The issues must ultimately be resolved by arts teachers themselves. *The Intelligence of Feeling* could well provide the basis for their discussions and the language that would enable them to discern both what they had in common and in what respects they were essentially different. The result could be a vigorous and concerted assertion by arts teachers of their crucial role in the education of young people, supported by evidence of a new sense of purpose and relevance in their work to the undoubted benefit of the whole of the secondary-school curriculum.

Our view of the educational function of the arts is not in itself new. Arts teachers have always placed strong emphasis upon the value of arts education as a means of self-expression and a stimulus to personal development. But these concepts have not hitherto been well understood and in consequence have failed to provide the arts curriculum with an essential organizing principle. The purpose of *The Intelligence of Feeling* is to reassure arts teachers of the legitimacy of their long-standing concern with *feeling* and to help them grasp the creative process through which the intelligence of feeling finds expression in the language of form.

A conceptual framework is presented which distinguishes between subject and object knowing, expressive and impressive action. It is based upon the notion, painstakingly developed in the opening section of the book, that all action is 'projection through a medium'. Expressive action is the projection of an expressive impulse through an expressive medium – such action constitutes subject knowing. Expressive action is the means by which an individual comes to know the world of his own feelings, of his own being – 'a world that exists only because he exists'. Impressive action is its exact counterpart and provides the individual with the means of knowing the world of objects – 'the world that exists whether or not he exists'. Subject knowing is *subject–reflexive action*: *feeling impulse* projected through an *expressive medium* yields *feeling form*. Subject–reflexive action is proposed as the common experiential root from which all the arts spring – subject knowing is their common goal.

57

Robert Witkin insists upon the crucial distinction between what he calls 're-flexive' and what he calls 'reactive' behaviour. In reactive expression the emotional impulse is merely discharged: the experience is such that the individual wishes simply to be released from it and his behaviour is designed to bring the tension down as quickly as possible. Acts of vandalism and tantrums are certainly expressive, but they are merely reactive and the actor, in achieving separation from his feelings, sacrifices the opportunity of working them through and coming to know and assimilate them. In the popular mind all forms of expressive behaviour have come to have this character and the expressive arts, both in school and out, are often felt to be extremely dangerous both to personal order and the social order. However, there is another form of expressive behaviour: behaviour that is reflexive rather than reactive. The distinction lies in the individual's holding on to his feelings and finding a means of engaging with them rather than simply releasing himself from them. This engagement is achieved by working the feelings through an expressive medium provided from and located in the world of objects. This, in effect, is what every artist does. He chooses a medium that he feels will adequately respond to his attempts to externalize, to embody his feelings. He engages in a reciprocating relationship with his medium, his consciousness oscillating between his own expressive impulse and the expressive response of the medium. The process results in a 'feeling form' that recalls his sensing and allows him to 'know his being'.

We suggest that the most critical aspect of arts teaching is the nature and purpose of the relationship between teacher and pupil within what Robert Witkin calls 'the educational encounter'. Expressive work in many arts departments sometimes means little more than 'letting them get on with it' – and such *laissez-faire* has attracted not a little scepticism to work bearing this description. This is an extremely unfortunate matter since it is precisely upon the pupil's expressive action that we should like to see the emphasis of any new arts curriculum placed – albeit rooted in a much more active and more stringent conception of the teacher's role in the learning process.

The basic elements of subject–reflexive action are the individual's feelings and his chosen medium of expression. Each of the arts offers a different medium – some, a combination of media. The critical problem for the 'artist' – whether a professional working in his studio or a child in a classroom – is medium control. We will assume that the artist has something to say – has an expressive impulse adequate to sustain his endeavour – otherwise he will merely produce empty form. (There has to be some necessity, some urgency about his commitment to his own expressive action.) We will further assume that the medium is one over which he has an effective degree of technical mastery or he will soon be frustrated in his bid to realize the expressive impulse in a feeling form that recalls it. Con-

58

trol of the medium in Robert Witkin's sense is not simply a technical problem. For him there are two alternatives – one that he calls 'rule-directed' control, and the other 'reflexive' control. Again 'reflexive' is the key word. It is, of course, perfectly possible to write a poem or a song, to make a drawing or deliver a speech according to the rules – of custom, aesthetics or whatever – to build form on the outside. But such an approach does not require the reciprocal interaction between impulse and its effect in the medium. The essential feature of reflexive control is that the process be guided throughout by the sensate impulse itself.

The consummation of the creative act, then, lies in the realization of feeling through the release of expressive impulse. It follows from what has been said that we are entirely in accord with those artists and art teachers who in recent years have been questioning the supremacy of the art product (the object or the performance), and have come to see the creative process itself as of much more educational significance. Concern for ways of knowing as distinct from bodies of knowledge is, of course, by no means confined to the arts curriculum.

In the final chapter of *The Intelligence of Feeling*, Robert Witkin formulates what he holds to be the three 'invariant' phases of the creative process and gives some guidance to the teacher as to how to enter the expressive act of the child and assist its development 'from within'. These he designates:

The setting of the sensate problem

The teacher enters the creative process by selecting and stimulating an appropriate sensate problem – that is to say, he makes sure that there is an impulse within the child to motivate and guide his expressive action. Of the sensate problem Robert Witkin writes that quite simply, all sensate disturbance whether great or small, pleasant or unpleasant, is a problem in so far as it makes demands upon us to structure our particularity.

He then proposes a tentative and intriguing model to account for the child's developing structural capacities in the realm of feelings and, in the light of that model, suggests the criteria which should determine a teacher's selection of appropriate sensate problems. The problem cannot be regarded as having been set, he says, until its structural character (contrast, dialectic or harmony for instance) is a felt experience of some intensity.

The making of a holding form . . .

that will 'encapsulate only the essential movement of the sensate impulse and . . . hold that movement in consciousness for the duration of the expressive act . . . a form that captures the structural characteristics [of the impulse] in their barest essentials. It is the essential gestalt of the disturbance that is held in the holding form'.

The purpose of making a holding form is to enable the pupils to maintain contact with the original impulse in the ensuing creative action. Once the impulse is lost then all hope of resolving the original problem in feeling form is lost too.

The movement through successive approximations to a resolution
. . . in which the pupil 'progresses from gross to refined control of the medium' in respect of the original sensate problem he seeks to resolve.

The process, inevitably only crudely outlined here, is elaborated and illustrated in the closing pages of *The Intelligence of Feeling* and is, arguably, the book's own crowning achievement. It carries over the theoretical insights of the work as a whole into the applied field and offers a positive basis upon which a revitalized curriculum in the arts could be raised. How would such a curriculum be evaluated? Ultimately in terms of the pupil's personal development. Progress would be measured in terms of the complexity of the sensate problems the pupil could handle. The elaboration of the world of sensate experience for the pupil would constitute personal development in the most intimate sense possible: the making of his feeling response in respect of 'the world in which he has his being'. And the art teacher's job is 'to make possible an adequate feeling response' to life and to living.

Secondary schools are relatively successful in promoting our understanding of and competence in the world of objects – indeed the bulk of the curriculum is geared to that purpose. However, much less is known of the way we order subjective experience – still less of the means by which the individual can be helped in building a coherent world of personal feeling. There is mounting concern today about the motivation and the attitudes of young people in the schools and the favoured response seems to be the sophistication and elaboration of pastoral and counselling services. But such developments can offer only partial solutions. The life of feeling was never entirely amenable to admonition or advice – structures of feeling are built experientially, feeling yields to feeling, not to talk about feeling. It is precisely because they have always offered men the means of realizing their feelings, of finding their way within and so of possessing this world that is unique to each of us, that the arts are of such critical importance in the field of education. Those whose feelings are unintelligible to them are as assuredly handicapped in the regulating of their lives as those others who are unable to think coherently and who can make little sense of the world they share with other men. Robert Witkin puts it thus:

> If the price of finding oneself in the world is that of losing the world in oneself, then the price is more than anyone can afford.

60

IV. Epilogue – the project in perspective

In concluding this report we draw into focus a number of recent developments in the two complementary fields from which this project has emanated: the arts and the curriculum. I think our study will come to be seen as having been very much of its time.

The arts

As I have already suggested, in the last ten years or so we have seen considerable activity in that area which lies between the worlds of the professional artist and the professional teacher. There has been a restlessness among many artists who have become dissatisfied with traditional forms and predictable responses. During this period a powerful assault has been made in some quarters upon the boundaries that have divided one art from another. The arts have literally taken to the roads, to the factory, the village hall and street corner as never before in modern times and we are witnessing something of a return to the days of the wandering player, the minstrel and the poet who speak directly to a small company of men, women and children. While it is certainly true that interest in the classical and traditional also continues to grow, what is rather more significant for our purpose is the sudden mushroom growth of smaller, private enterprises. Some have overt social or political objectives while others are less directive, more personal and more easy-going. This resurgence of artistic activity at the grass roots of our society throughout Europe and America, the dramatic demands for 'live' contact, has undoubtedly had many causes. It is clearly something of a reaction against the mechanistic quality of life and leisure today; it marks a strongly felt need by artist and audience for direct interaction, for engagement with experience that is immediate and personal. Despite commercial exploitation the movement remains basically anti-consumerist in its inspiration. Nor is it by any means restricted to the young. Its aims are genuinely re-creative.

Growing public concern for the quality of modern life is evidenced in the attention now being given at local government, national and international levels to the question of cultural policies (for example, the Council of Europe's Ten Towns Project). And it is becoming increasingly recognized that the arts have an important social role, not just as the leisure interest of a privileged élite, but as an

61

essential element of lifelong education. The Arts and the Adolescent Project arose naturally in such a climate and, though it has always had something of a struggle to survive, there was an inevitability about its inception. Perhaps its most unusual feature was the critical involvement of a social scientist.

If we take a bird's eye view of arts education for a moment, and in particular of that shadowy border country that lies beyond the school, we shall notice much that is exciting and encouraging.

Art is now taught in every school in the country – primary and secondary; music and drama in one form or another are also widespread. There has been a considerable increase in the number of candidates offering art and music at advanced-level GCE, and new school buildings are often designed with the needs of the arts subjects well understood. Testifying to a growing interest in the arts, local authorities are steadily increasing their specialist advisory staff. Some gave a clear lead long ago and have now established a reputation for outstanding work in the arts in their schools.

We have studied the entries for O- and A-level examinations for the period 1935 to 1967. The number of entries in arts subjects has increased greatly as part of an overall increase in entries. But, at A level, the increase in art and in music is greater than would be expected:

Percentage of all entries		
	1935	1967
Music	0·1	0·6
Art	0·3	0·4

The number of entries was easier to locate than the number of candidates, but the limited information on candidates indicates a fairly stable percentage offering art/music at O level and a substantial increase in the percentage offering art/music at A level. This evidence can be seen either as a positive sign of the extension of arts teaching, or as a depressing indication of the pressure to measure and quantify in a way which may be inappropriate for arts subjects.

In different parts of the country specially-equipped arts centres* have been established, and these offer teachers and their pupils resources and opportunities of which they have been quick to take advantage. Judging from the numbers of schools recommended to us as remarkable for their work in the arts, it would probably be fair to assert that there are more good teachers at work in our schools today than ever before, many of them bringing to their schools a new breadth and liberality of outlook – linking their pupils with the artistic resources

* For example, the Inner London Education Authority's 'Cockpit', the Midlands Arts Centre (in Birmingham) and Devon's Beaford Centre.

of the local community. Schools are visited not only by musicians and actors but by poets and writers,* artists and craftsmen – many of whom, like the actor-teacher for instance, are ready to work with the children. Also there has recently been a vigorous growth of opportunity for young people to follow up and develop their interests in the arts outside the school, continuing after they have left. Art colleges open their doors to youngsters after school hours; teachers, students, youth leaders and artists themselves give up their evenings, weekends and holidays to work in drama workshops, music centres and in the clubs.

There is a widespread commitment among many contemporary artists to make their art serve the community – in immediate and direct terms. The spirit of the Bauhaus is very much alive and can be detected in a variety of situations in which the young are involved with the living arts.

In *Concerning the Spiritual in Art* (Wittenborn, 1947), Kandinsky spoke thus of the role of art and the vocation of the artist:

Not only is art simultaneously the echo and mirror [of contemporary feeling] but it possesses also an awakening prophetic power which can have far-reaching and profound effects.

The spiritual life to which art belongs, and of which it is one of the mightiest agents, is a complex but definite movement above and beyond, which can be translated into simplicity. This movement is that of cognition. Although it may take different forms, it holds basically to the same internal meaning and purpose.

The causes of the necessity to move forward and upward – through sweat, suffering, evil and torments – are obscure. When a stage has been reached at which obstacles have been cleared from the way, a hidden, malevolent hand scatters new obstacles. The path often seems blocked or destroyed. But someone always comes to the rescue – someone like ourselves in everything, but with a secretly implanted power of 'vision'. He sees and points out. This high gift (often a heavy burden)† at times he would gladly relinquish. But he cannot. Scorned and disliked, he drags the heavy weight of resisting humanity forward and upward.

It is, in the context of the present discussion concerning the 'instrumentality' or social purposefulness of art, not inappropriate to draw further upon the views of the Bauhaus teachers – all of whom, at the conscious level at least, were committed to the idea of the artist's working within and engaging with his society rather

* A Department of Education and Science memorandum issued in December 1969 lists the names and addresses of writers who are willing to visit schools and colleges to talk about their work and that of other writers, and to discuss subjects of common interest.

† See A. Alvarez, *The Savage God* (Weidenfeld & Nicolson, 1971).

than remaining aloof from it. He should exert all his technical and aesthetic skills and his moral and political awareness to influence the development of our technological environment. In his *Apollo in Democracy: the Cultural Obligation of the Architect* (McGraw-Hill, 1968), Walter Gropius condemned the idea of the 'professional artist':

> Architects, sculptors, painters, we must all turn to the crafts. Art is not a 'profession'. There is no essential difference between the artist and the craftsman. In rare moments of inspiration, moments beyond the control of his will, the grace of heaven may cause his work to blossom into art. But proficiency in his craft is essential to every artist . . . This world of drawing and painting, of designers and handicraft-artists must at last become a building world again.

Moholy-Nagy struck a warmer note when he said that although he had seen in emotion only a precious individual barrier against the group, he had learned differently. Perhaps because he had been a teacher so long that he had come to see emotion as the great adhesive, the ray that goes out to warm, and the response that comes back and confirms.

It is this spirit which animates and sustains two relatively new attempts to turn the arts to broadly educational ends by giving them a social or therapeutic role. They are peripheral to our necessarily rather sharply focused study of arts education, but both deserve attention and support. The Arts Council of Great Britain recently allocated money for what it called 'special activities'. Some of these ventures are little more than haphazard, personal gestures; others have attracted the support of local and national bodies. The inspiration behind this vigorous grass-roots movement is evident in the following piece, written by Wendy Harpe:

> The majority of people possess, no matter how unused, real creative and imaginative faculties . . . In terms of the arts it is unfortunate that in practice it is often ideas of what is art . . . that prevent people from using their creative faculties.*

An account of the Great George's Project in Liverpool by Bill Harpe* brings the concept to life. The activities of Ed Berman's Inter-Action Trust have a different emphasis, but spring from the same commitment: to make the arts relevant in an immediate, personal way, and to set the artist to work in the community itself. Albert Hunt wrote an appraisal of Berman's work in *New Society* (26 June 1969):

* Wendy Harpe, 'Arts and the community', and Bill Harpe, 'The Great George's Project', in A. Schouvaloff (ed.), *Place for the Arts* (North Western Arts Association, Seel House Press, 1970).

What is Berman doing in these sessions? It seems to me that he is not just developing verbal and imaginative skills. He is creating a sense of personal responsibility. And he tries to extend that same sense outside the sessions.

A sense of personal responsibility – the insistence that to make a personal response is the most elementary affirmation of the life of the individual, and that to accept responsibility for his own life is his only hope – and ours. Robert Witkin's *The Intelligence of Feeling* has the same thrust.

Education

So too, within the curriculum field, the direction our work has taken is in keeping with the spirit of the age. The Arts and the Adolescent Project is part of a comprehensive national effort in the field of curriculum development, an effort that has been paralleled all over Europe as educational systems have become subject to rapid expansion.* The immediate incentive here in England has been the raising of the statutory school-leaving age which, together with the growing tendency for more pupils to stay on at school because they want to, has meant a dramatic increase in the size of the school population.

It was fairly anticipated at the outset that R o S L A would create problems for the schools, as Joslyn Owen indicated in the *Higher Education Journal*:

> . . . raising the school leaving age is resented by many parents (and pupils) and is a subject of trepidation for some teachers. Add the lack of interest felt, not only for school subjects but for school itself, by the present fifteen-year-old leaver . . . Add the fact that curriculum theory does not exist in this country, that we do not know what factors within schools support or hinder curriculum change, and that we do not know, on the whole, what is either the objective or the effectiveness of much teaching within existing curricula. (summer 1968, p. 10)

From a limited commitment to help teachers meet some of these questions the curriculum development movement has in recent years broadened and deepened its concerns. Individual projects, increasingly, have had to take account not simply of the early leaver or the below-average pupil but of the total school population.

We found that we could not accept the implication in our terms of reference that the general situation in the schools could be improved simply in terms of the transference and piece-meal adaptation of methods, and the deployment of

* See Saul B. Robinsohn, 'A conceptual structure of curriculum development', *Comparative Education*, vol. 5 (December 1969), pp. 221–8 – paper to fourth biennial meeting of Comparative Education Society in Europe, the general theme of which was 'Curriculum development in Europe at the second level of education'.

materials that particular teachers had deemed successful. Underlying the questions of what to teach and how to teach it lies the most fundamental question of all: why? It became increasingly clear to us that where the arts curriculum was concerned this question simply could not be begged. All discussion of content, methods, materials and organization hinged upon a satisfactory account being given of the function of the arts in the education of children in school. Our three-year study has been organized in an attempt to set out a working hypothesis which arts teachers might test and modify in the light of their own experience.

What we have called 'a conceptual framework' is of course essential not just to an arts curriculum but to all curricula. Such a framework has taken time to evolve and had to be supported by research. Our approach inevitably proved unpopular in some quarters. We found ourselves agreeing, however, with OECD's *Modernising our Schools: Curriculum Improvement and Educational Development* (Paris, 1966) which points out:

> Educational policy is determined by all kinds of factors except the results of research. At best, *ad hoc* research is called upon to help clarify particular details of policy decisions, or, *post factum*, to determine the particularities of the implementation. In many cases this state of affairs is more the result of a traditional attitude towards policy making than of the absence of research evidence. It is, however, obvious that both factors are intimately related: good research compels policy makers to revise the bases of their decision-making, a favourable political climate is liable to create better conditions for research . . .

The report concludes by insisting on 'the need to make research the real centre of gravity of educational policy and educational practice'.

We saw the project's purpose as contributing to an informed discussion of their role in education among arts educators themselves. We aimed to help them think about arts education in terms of the function of the arts in the experience of young people. Our work has necessarily been of a 'back room' nature. Any new arts curriculum is still a long way off. We needed a yardstick by which to judge the effectiveness of the old before we could begin to design an alternative for the future. A lengthy and searching dialogue is now called for, and a whole programme of curriculum experiment will be necessary in order that the practical implications of the project's work may be fully realized.

In his 'Methodology of evaluation', Scriven* has pointed out that

> The educational profession is suffering from a completely inappropriate conception of the cost scale for educational research. To develop a new

* In R. W. Tyler, R. M. Gagné and M. Scriven, *Perspectives of Curriculum Evaluation.* AERA Monographs on Curriculum Evaluation, No. 1 (Rand McNally, Chicago, 1967), p.83.

automobile engine or rocket engine is a very, very expensive business . . .* There have been numerous and longstanding proposals to the effect that the support for educational research and development should be at least 1% of total educational budgets. Yet the 1960 figure for the U.S. has only 0·12% and the 1965 figure 0·22%. By contrast, the more dynamic industrials in the U.S. spend up to 10% of their turnover on research and development, to improve their products and production process. Indeed a single major chemical firm is reported to be spending $110 million a year on research – which is more than is spent in the entire nation on educational research.

We would argue that the profession is also completely unrealistic about the time scale, not just for educational research but for any specific programme of curriculum development. A new curriculum is a highly complex product which takes not only money but time to develop. This is a concept which is neither accepted by nor acceptable to the profession at present. Given the prevailing sense of crisis and the backlog of complacency and inactivity, of years in which the basis of the school curriculum went unquestioned, this is perhaps not surprising. However, precipitate action has already strengthened the reactionary cause and the whole basis of the progressive movement in education has recently been called in question. As J. Lauwerys warns in his *Teachers and Teaching* (Evans, 1969), curriculum development has become 'a hit and miss affair'. He writes of

Vague wholesale programmes of reform that . . . have failed to materialize in practice; of the too ready acceptance of the reactionaries by educators. Disapproval of change is symptomatic of a certain point of view. It is often fortified by the chaos that follows reform based on slogans rather than in sound theory.

Professor William Taylor spoke about educational change in his inaugural lecture, *Half a Million Teachers* (University of Bristol Institute of Education, 1968):

In an occupation such as teaching, the choice in the years ahead is not between stability and change but between, on the one hand, change which is understood, and, where possible, planned and controlled, and on the other a series of hasty and ill-contrived adaptations to the march of events. In this process the part played by those who are concerned with educational study in the university is not so much with the how as with the why; it is essentially a critical activity, an attempt to help get the right questions asked and to indicate some of the pitfalls that need to be avoided in trying to

* In this connexion see also P. H. Coombs, *The World Educational Crisis: a Systems Analysis* (Oxford University Press, 1968).

answer them. In the terms suggested by R. M. Hutchins, the task of a professional school within a university is not only to prepare people for the profession, but chiefly to criticise the profession.

It is obvious that the real development work remains to be done *by the teachers*: those with specialized experience of arts education.

We would argue that curriculum renewal has to be based upon what has been called 'rolling research' and we see this as the proper function of a university-based project. We are hopeful that the quality of subsequent discussion and of eventual curriculum action will vindicate our approach, and that our particular contribution will be of use to 'the practising educators'.

Arts education begins and ends with people, not with products or performances. Qualitative problem solving in the world of objects must find its ultimate relevance in the lives of human beings, in the quality of personal relationships. We need to know more about the source and dynamics of human emotional life. We must find more effective ways of helping people meet and solve problems that arise in connexion with the quality of their lives. It is our view that 'talking about' is of distinctly limited value in this area – what we are concerned to develop is an increasingly complex emotional apparatus to complement a man's sophisticated intellect. Upon the range, depth and adaptability of that apparatus (the intelligence of feeling) will depend the quality of a man's life – his sense of commitment of his work, his ability to find and sustain satisfying relationships in varying degrees of closeness to himself, ultimately his feeling for life itself – *his* life.

It is our hypothesis that the arts offer us – not so much as product but as process – a vital instrument in the education of the feelings. Robert Witkin has been developing a model of emotional behaviour: in essence he is suggesting that the dynamics of the aesthetic experience, the characteristics of artistic form, are the very dynamics of the emotional life itself, expressed and embodied – to use Suzanne Langer's term – in 'perceptible form'. By bringing children to confront and 'solve' problems in their own immediate, qualitative experience, problems in sound, image and movement, we hope to promote the development of structures of feeling which make them not necessarily successful artists or even discriminating patrons of the arts but people whose humanity is demonstrated by the ways in which their sympathy flows, by the meaning for each of them of their own life of feeling. The arts curriculum must have its roots in the immediate sensory experience of the individual. Its starting-point must be the re-sensitizing and re-training of the senses themselves: the basic source of perception. Active participation would be its hallmark: music education, for instance, would be – as in many schools it already is – music-making and dancing.

The experience that we wish to encourage and develop in our schools bears the stamp of the creative act itself. We do not wish to produce more performers but more composers, more creators. We wish all children to find the arts *useful*, in Suzanne Langer's sense, in providing 'perceptible form expressive of their own feelings'. They will seek their own forms, and struggle to adapt themselves so as to make use of forms developed by other people. The experience is a restless one – carrying them from points of balance and of insight into doubt and confusion as, first of all, the new problem in feeling is fixed, and then hopefully resolved in form. What we shall be developing is not knowledge about art, but experience of the arts as ways of knowing – ways of nurturing and of developing the life of the feelings.

The drive to go on from solution to problem (the divine restlessness George Herbert wrote about) – the necessarily problematic quality of all experience – is the need to retain control of one's relationship with the environment. The life-loving (aesthetic) person is aware of the torrent that threatens to overwhelm him. He needs to keep moving in order to stand still. The 'living-dead' are bowled along downstream, undistressed because unconscious – anaesthetized. The hope for a man is this strenuous standing still, this mastery (always precarious) of the environment – the transient ordering of chaos and the defending of new territories. We must not surrender this hope, this concept of human potential. Education serves to realize human capacity by increasing competence: so men may find, in themselves and in others, a *human* use for human beings.

To exercise this self-control – to act in control – is to affirm one's own being, one's own identity. It is to actualize the self, and the ensuing gratification is a spur to further such acting, self-actualizing. Security of identity is this very 'standing still' in the torrent. One looks therefore for opportunities for self-actualization through work, through personal relationships, and through play. We should also expect the experience offered to young people in school to be of the same quality, having as its end the self-actualizing of the individual.

In advocating that we give a place in education to artistic activity as I have been describing it, I think it right to point out that I am not recommending an innocuous or merely pleasurable activity. I am not thinking of hobbies – nor yet of the life of the professional artist. We may or may not agree with the view that Henry Moore holds – that art is more concerned with power than beauty. At all events the arts challenge, disturb, put us at risk. Kenneth Tynan has claimed that it was characteristic of the arts that they went too far. In his *Tropic of Cancer*, Henry Miller makes a similar point when reproving Ravel for mistaking intellectual for aesthetic form and ultimately failing in the shape of his *Bolero*:

> I thought when the drums started it would go on forever. I expected to see people fall out of the boxes or throw their hats away. There was something

69

heroic about it and he could have driven us stark mad, Ravel, if he had wanted to. But that's not Ravel. Suddenly it all died down . . . He arrested himself. A great mistake in my humble opinion. Art consists in going to the full length. If you start with the drums you have to end with dynamite, TNT . . .

Emotion is indeed the life of art and, while being wary, we should not be afraid of it. But I do not want to suggest that the power I am speaking of is either mere emotionalism or frenzy. The power of art to disturb us – to cause us to re-make our images of the world and of ourselves – is more subtle, more complex than this. The traditional image of the artist and of art as potentially powerful disruptive influences is not for nothing and if it is art we want in education then we must acknowledge (and see that everyone else understands) that it is dynamite and not firecrackers that we are offering the young. The process, the experience of art, is of value to man primarily because it has its own way of rebuilding him at the same time as it seems to undermine and blow him at the sky. In arguing for the arts in education I should not wish to argue for a conception less dramatic: nor, because the emotional impulse is constrained and shaped by the medium in which it takes form, a conception less disciplined.

The point of art in education is that involvement with art means engagement with the problematic in one's own emotional experience.

In order to arrive there,

To arrive where you are, to get from where you are not,
　You must go by a way wherein there is no ecstasy.
In order to arrive at what you do not know
　You must go by a way which is the way of ignorance.
In order to possess what you do not possess
　You must go by way of dispossession.
In order to arrive at what you are not
　You must go through the way in which you are not.
And what you do not know is the only thing you know
And what you own is what you do not own
And where you are is where you are not.

T. S. ELIOT 'East Coker' (Four Quartets)

Appendices

Appendix A The arts and the handicapped*

So diverse are the activities of arts therapists – as we have discovered in the programme of visits and personal interviews we have undertaken during the six
months allowed for this study – that it is no simple matter to reduce this experience to a simple statement or formula. In essence arts therapists use the experience of art in the interests of healing. Their work ranges widely both in terms of
the aims and ambitions of arts therapists themselves and also in the degree of
importance attached to it by their colleagues and by those responsible for
managing the institutions in which the physically, mentally and emotionally
handicapped are cared for.

Broadly speaking, the arts are used therapeutically as a means of diagnosis, as
a re-creative activity, and for specifically curative purposes. As will become clear
from this brief introduction to the field, most arts therapists are engaged in re-
creative activities. Few value the use of a patient's art work for diagnostic purposes and this is currently a controversial question. It is impossible to speak of
cure but rather of change or growth, especially since so many patients and pupils
with whom the arts therapist works are physically incurable. Instead the therapist aims to help each individual to recognize and come to terms with his handi-
cap and his environment and to develop to his full potential. A great deal of what
we have seen and learned in the course of our inquiry testifies to the remarkable
impact arts therapists are currently making upon life in our hospitals and special
schools.

In some hospitals the activities of the arts therapist may be carefully integrated
into a total programme of therapeutic and medical/psychiatric care, in others,
less happily, the arts therapist may have to work very much on the periphery and
in considerable isolation. Ideally the arts therapist operates as a member of a
therapeutic team headed by a consultant psychiatrist, presenting case reports on
each patient to meetings of the whole staff. However, with only one consultant
for every 110 mentally-ill patients and one for every 486 subnormal patients,

* Summary of a special study by Juliet Megee, appointed to the project to study the
therapeutic use of the arts.

71

such an arrangement is, necessarily, the exception rather than the rule. In special schools, versatility tends to be more prized than specialized knowledge or skill, and it is rare that an arts therapist is given the support and consideration that are perhaps necessary if his efforts are really to bear fruit.

Conditions of work are, by and large, far from ideal. This is particularly the case for therapists working in hospitals. Of British mental hospitals 65 per cent were built before 1891 and over 40 per cent are more than a hundred years old. Many of these hospitals have to contend with serious overcrowding (15 per cent of the mentally ill and 25 per cent of subnormal patients are in wards of fifty beds or more – often with a space of less than 2 feet between beds). One drama therapist spoke of his difficulties in these terms:

> The conditions under which my current work is attempted entail sharing rooms with various other people and activities in remote parts of a vast, sprawling building which necessitates a considerable amount of movement for patients who sometimes find walking difficult. Since each patient has to be collected and returned to his or her ward, this involves almost as much time shuffling up and down corridors as engaging in therapeutic activities of a more imaginative nature. Attempts to make various rooms in which I have been put to work more congenial in appearance are thwarted by the hospital's standard of hygiene which insists that a room is not fit to be occupied unless it is bare. When patients enter such a room, they enter the familiar preconditioned environment that in so many cases is all they know and understand. The ability to establish new modes of perception and methods of relating in such an environment is severely handicapped by their conditioning.

It is the exceptional school or hospital that is able to provide a specially-equipped place for the arts therapist to work in – most have to work with very limited resources in circumstances that threaten to invalidate the essential quality of the experience that the therapist is aiming to create. In very large hospitals (some carry over 2000 patients) it is impossible to attend to everyone adequately, and the therapist has to decide between offering a limited recreational service for the greatest number and working only in the hospital school and with the small number of patients who may be referred by the psychiatrist. It is the experience of many arts therapists, both in schools and hospitals, that their sessions come to be regarded as useful dumping grounds for difficult pupils and patients and, though some of them are happy to accept the challenge, it is easy to appreciate that others might regard such treatment as evidence of the lack of a true understanding of their work. The arts therapist, not unlike his counter-

72

part in the schools, is often a very vulnerable member of staff, subject to the whim and all too dependent upon the patronage of his superiors.

Arts therapists work with adults and children suffering from a wide range of handicaps. For some of their patients there can be no hope of a normal life and the therapist must expect little more than a momentary flicker of understanding or attention by way or response. For most patients the arts therapist will be able to contribute significantly towards bringing about a fuller, richer and more personally responsible life – even though society may continue to find it difficult to accept them. Many patients are multi-handicapped, and problems of emotional and social adjustment inevitably arise as a result of their disabilities.

It is essentially in the realm of the feelings that the arts therapist works, introducing the patient to an inner world the existence of which he has perhaps only dimly sensed, providing him with a coherent outlet for experiences and feelings that he is unable to assimilate or express in any other way. Thus, the arts therapist aims to make his patient aware of his potential to develop towards involvement and participation in a world outside himself and his limitations, building up his confidence to make meaningful contributions in group situations where possible, and giving him the personal satisfaction of tangible success in areas where there are no ideal solutions to be vainly striven for. However, where such aims conflict with the orientation of the institution in which he is working (one that perhaps pursues a purely custodial policy or offers support only through drugs or electro-convulsive therapy) it is difficult to see his efforts having any real prospect of success.

All art forms can be initially and enjoyably experienced as play and even the most severely handicapped can gain pleasure and satisfaction from handling materials such as clay and finger paints, jostling a tree hung with bells with any part of their bodies, sliding across the floor, having a quartz crystal brushed against their cheeks, being rocked gently to and fro by their companions. Of course a great deal of arts activity goes a long way beyond such primitive experience, but one cannot overestimate the value of even this most elementary activity for some of the patients whose needs the arts therapist must seek to satisfy.

The therapist sets out to find and make contact with the patient 'where he is' and then to present him with a relaxed situation in which he feels free: free from a sense of being assessed and found wanting, free to push back the frontiers of possibility and arrive at a new sense of his own value.

We have met with countless instances of arts therapists bringing their patients to a new level of self-respect through personal achievement in the experience of art and, frequently, simply through the close, personal attention that the arts therapist tries to give to each patient. This story is very revealing in what it

73

suggests of the potential of this kind of experience for human beings whose personal resources have been so severely curtailed.

> A group of young children at a school for the cerebral-palsied were improvising the theme of Brecht's *Caucasian Chalk Circle*. A child, who could not walk but could slither, 'snaked in' the circle in the court scene, all the time demanding patience 'I'm coming your worship . . . yes, your majesty . . . just a minute . . .'

The arts therapist has a positive purpose. It is not to encourage a withdrawal from reality, a self-forgetting, but rather – by refusing merely to cosset or amuse – to set genuine problems in experience and help their patients to deal with them. They seek to stimulate acts of recognition and recreation. Most arts therapists seek, wherever possible, to bring about some measure of development in terms of their patient's adaptation to the subjective world within and the objective world without. Progress must in many cases be tragically slight – but important gains are often made. As one headmaster said to us,

> When trying to cope with maladjusted boys one of the most difficult obstacles to overcome is that of convincing them that they are worth-while human beings. Most, if not all, have a very low opinion of their own intrinsic value.

Our survey has indicated, however, the rich potential for personal expression and achievement offered by the arts to people whose handicaps have so severely restricted their opportunities of self-realization and so reduced their scope for personal fulfilment. The Seebohm Report offers the following assessment of the situation as far as young people are concerned:

> *At least* one child in ten in the population will need special educational, psychiatric or social help before it reaches the age of 18 . . . at present *at most* one child in twenty-two is receiving such help.*

* *Report of the Committee on Local Authority and Allied Personal Social Services* (HMSO, 1968), para. 173.

74

Appendix B Bibliography*

Arts education

English

ABBS, PETER, *English for Diversity*. Heinemann Educational, 1969.

BARNES, DOUGLAS, BRITTON, JAMES, ROSEN, HAROLD and the London Association for the Teaching of English, *Language, the Learner and the School*. Penguin Books, 1969.

BECKETT, JACK, *The Keen Edge*. Blackie, 1965.

CLEGG, A. B., *The Excitement of Writing*. Chatto & Windus, 1964.

CREBER, J. W. P., *Sense and Sensitivity*. University of London Press, 1965.

CUTFORTH, J. A. and BATTERSBY, S. H., *Children and Books*. Blackwell, 1962.

FISHER, MARGERY, *Intent upon Reading*. Brockhampton Press, 1964.

FOWLER, F. D., *Language and Emotion*. Longman, 1966.

HOLBROOK, DAVID, *The Exploring World*. Cambridge University Press, 1967.

HOLBROOK, DAVID, *The Secret Places*. Methuen, 1964.

HOLBROOK, DAVID, *English for the Rejected*. Cambridge University Press, 1964.

HOLBROOK, DAVID, *English for Maturity*. Cambridge University Press, 1961.

HOURD, M. L., *Some Emotional Aspects of Learning*. Heinemann Educational, 1951.

JACKSON, BRIAN, *English versus Examinations*. Chatto & Windus, 1965.

MATTAM, DONALD, *The Vital Approach*. Macmillan, 1963.

MARLAND, MICHAEL, *Towards the New Fifth*. Longman, 1969.

OWENS, GRAHAM and MARLAND, MICHAEL (eds), *The Practice of English Teaching*. Blackie, 1970.

STEINER, GEORGE, *Language and Silence*. Penguin Books, 1969.

STEVENS, FRANCES, *English and Examinations*. Hutchinson Educational, 1970.

STEVENS, ROY, *An Approach to Literature*. Longman, 1966.

SUMMERFIELD, GEOFFREY and TUNNICLIFFE, STEVEN (eds), *English in Practice*. Cambridge University Press, 1971.

THOMPSON, DENYS and JACKSON, BRIAN, *English in Education*. Chatto & Windus, 1962.

WALSH, J. H., *Teaching English*. Heinemann Educational, 1965.

WHITEHEAD, FRANK, *The Disappearing Dais*. Chatto & Windus, 1966.

WILKINSON, ANDREW, *The Foundations of Language*. Oxford University Press, 1971.

* Based on a bibliography specially compiled for the project by Alma Craft.

Art

BARKAN, MANUEL, 'Transition in art education – changing conceptions of curriculum content and teaching', *Art Education*, **XV**, October 1962, 12–18.

BARKAN, MANUEL, CHAPMAN, L. H. and KERN, E. J., *Guidelines*. CEMREL, St Ann, Miss., 1970.

CHURCHILL, A. R., *Art for Preadolescents*. McGraw-Hill, 1971.

Department of Education and Science, *Art in Schools* (Education Survey 11). HMSO, 1971.

EISNER, E. W. 'Toward a new era in art education', *Studies in Art Education*, **6**, spring 1965, 54–62.

EISNER, E. W., 'Art education' in *Encyclopedia of Educational Research*, ed. Robert L. Ebel. Collier-Macmillan, 4th edn, 1969, 76-86.

EISNER, E. W., *Readings in Art Education*. Blaisdell, 1966.

FIELD, DICK, *Change in Art Education*. Routledge & Kegan Paul, 1970.

HANNEMA, SJOERD, *Fads, Fakes and Fantasies*. Macdonald, 1970.

HOGG, JAMES, *Psychology and the Visual Arts*. Penguin Books, 1969.

KELLOGG, RHODA, *Analysing Children's Art*. National Press Books, 1969.

KLEE, PAUL, *The Thinking Eye* (Notebooks, Vol. 1). Lund Humphries, 1961.

LANIER, VINCENT, *Teaching Secondary Art*. International Textbook, 1964.

MCFEE, J. K., *Preparation for Art*. Wadsworth Publishing, Belmont, California, 1961.

MANZELLA, DAVID, *Educationists and the Evisceration of the Visual Arts*. International Textbook, 1963.

MOHOLY-NAGY, LASZLO, *Painting, Photography, Film*. Lund Humphries, 1969.

MOHOLY-NAGY, LASZLO, *The New Vision*. Wittenborn, New York, 1947.

PALMER, FREDERICK, *Art and the Young Adolescent*. Pergamon, 1970.

PORTCHMOUTH, J., *Secondary School Art*. Studio Vista, 1971.

READ, SIR HERBERT, *Education through Art*. Faber, 1961.

RICHARDSON, MARION, *Art and the Child*. University of London Press, 1948.

ROWLAND, K., *Looking and Seeing*, Books 1–4 (with Teachers' Notes), Ginn, 1964.

SAUSMAREZ, MAURICE DE. *Basic Design*. Studio Vista, 1964.

Scottish Education Department, *Art in Secondary Schools*. HMSO, Edinburgh, 1971.

SMITH, R. A., *Aesthetics and Criticism in Art Education*. Rand McNally, 1966.

THOMPSON, D'ARCY, *On Growth and Form*. Cambridge University Press, 1966.

TSUGAWA, ALBERT, 'The nature of the aesthetic and human values', *Art Education*, **21**, November 1968, 9–15.

WEITZ, M., 'The nature of art' in *Readings in Art Education: a Primary Source Book*, ed. E. W. Eisner and D. W. Ecker. Xerox College Publishing, Lexington, Mass., 1966.

Drama

Arts Council of Great Britain, *The Provision of Theatre for Young People*. Arts Council, 1966.

CHILVER, PETER, *Improvised Drama*. Batsford, 1967.

Department of Education and Science, *Drama* (Education Survey 2). HMSO, 1968.

Department of Education and Science, 'Drama in education', *Reports on Education*, No. 50, November 1968.

DODD, NIGEL and HICKSON, WINIFRED, *Drama and Theatre in Education*. Heinemann Educational, 1971.

HEATHCOTE, DOROTHY, 'How does drama serve thinking, talking and writing?', *Elementary English*, **47**, December 1970, 1077–81.

HODGSON, JOHN and RICHARDS, ERNEST, *Improvisation: Discovery and Creativity in Drama*. Methuen, 1966.

PEMBERTON-BILLING, R. N. and CLEGG, J. D., *Teaching Drama*. University of London Press, 1965.

SLADE, PETER, *An Introduction to Child Drama*. University of London Press, 1967.

SLADE, PETER, *Experience of Spontaneity*. Longman, 1968.

SLADE, PETER, *Children's Theatre and Theatre for Young People*. Tom Stacey, 1969.

SLADE, PETER et al., 'The teaching of drama', *Higher Education Journal*, **17**, summer 1970, 10–26.

SLADE, PETER, *Drama and the Middle School:* report from Educational Drama Association for Schools Council Middle Years of Schooling Project. University of Lancaster Educational Drama Association, 1971.

WAY, BRIAN, *Development through Drama*. Longman, 1967.

Music

ALVIN, JULIETTE, *Music Therapy*. John Baker, 1966.

BROUDY, HARRY S., 'A realistic philosophy of music education', in *Basic Concepts in Music Education*, ed. Nelson B. Henry (57th Yearbook of the National Society for the Study of Education, Part I). University of Chicago Press, 1958, pp. 62–87.

DENNIS, BRIAN, *Experimental Music in Schools*. Oxford University Press, 1970.

Department of Education and Science, 'Music and the young', *Reports on Education*, No. 39, September 1967.

Department of Education and Science, *Music in Schools* (Pamphlet No. 27). HMSO, 2nd edn, 1969.

Department of Education and Science, 'Creative music in schools', *Reports on Education*, No. 63, April 1970.

DOBBS, J. P. B., *The Slow Learner and Music – A Handbook for Teachers*. Oxford University Press, 1966.

MELLERS, WILFRID, *Music and Society*. Dobson Books, 1946.

MELLERS, WILFRID, *Music in a New Found Land*. Barrie & Jenkins, 1964.

MELLERS, WILFRID, *Caliban Reborn – Renewal in 20th Century Music*. Gollancz, 1968.

NORDOFF, PAUL and ROBBINS, CLIVE, *Therapy in Music for Handicapped Children*. Gollancz, 1971.

PAYNTER, JOHN and ASTON, PETER, *Sound and Silence: Classroom Projects in Creative Music*. Cambridge University Press, 1970.

REIMER, BENNETT, 'A new curriculum for secondary general music', *Bulletin of the Council for Research in Music Education*, No. 4, winter 1965, 11–20.

SCHAFER, R. MURRAY, *The Composer in the Classroom*. BMI Canada, Toronto, Ontario, 1965.

SCHNEIDER, E., 'Music education' in *Encyclopedia of Educational Research*, ed. Robert L. Ebel. Collier-Macmillan, 4th edn, 1969, pp. 895–907.

Schools Council, *Music and the Young School Leaver* (Working Paper 35). Evans/Methuen Educational, 1971.

SWANWICK, KEITH, *Popular Music and the Teacher*. Pergamon, 1968.

Dance

LABAN, RUDOLF, *Modern Educational Dance*. Macdonald & Evans, 1964.

LABAN, RUDOLF, *The Mastery of Movement*. DBS Publications, New York, 1960/Macdonald & Evans, 1961.

NORTH, MARION, *Introduction to Movement Study and Teaching*. Macdonald & Evans, 1971.

RUSSELL, JOAN, *Modern Dance in Education*. Macdonald & Evans, 1958.

Film

ARNHEIM, RUDOLF, *Film as Art*. Faber, 1958.

British Film Institute, *The Cinema: A Short Booklist*. BFI Education Department.

British Film Institute, *Study of Film – A Survey of Approaches*. BFI, 1967–68.

LOWNDES, DOUGLAS, *Film Making in Schools*. Batsford, 1968.

TAYLOR, JOHN RUSSELL, *Cinema Eye, Cinema Ear*. Methuen, 1964.

Curriculum development

BLOOM, B. S. (ed.) *et al.*, *Taxonomy of Educational Objectives: the Classification of Educational Goals*, Handbook I: Cognitive Domain. Longmans Green, 1956.

KRATHWOHL, D. R., BLOOM, B. S., and MASIA, B. B. *Taxonomy of Educational Objectives: the Classification of Educational Goals*, Handbook II: Affective Domain. Longmans Green, 1964.

HIRST, P. H. and PETERS, R. S., *The Logic of Education*. Routledge & Kegan Paul, 1970.

HOOPER, RICHARD (ed.), *The Curriculum: Context, Design and Development* (Open University Set Book). Oliver & Boyd, Edinburgh, 1971.

MURDOCK, G. and PHELPS, G., *Mass Media and the Secondary School* (Schools Council Research Studies). Macmillan, 1973.

MUSGROVE, F., 'Curriculum Objectives', *Journal of Curriculum Studies*, **1**, November 1968, 5–18.

OECD, *Modernising our Schools: Curriculum Improvement and Educational Development*. Organization for Economic Co-operation and Development, Paris, 1966.

PHENIX, PHILIP H., *Realms of Meaning: a Philosophy of the Curriculum for General Education*. McGraw-Hill, 1964.

RICHMOND, W. K., *The School Curriculum*. Methuen, 1971.

ROBINSOHN, S., 'A conceptual structure of curriculum development', *Comparative Education*, **5**, December 1969, 221–8.

SCRIVEN, M., 'The methodology of evaluation' in *Perspectives of Curriculum Evaluation*, ed. R. W. Tyler, R. M. Gagné and M. Scriven (American Educational Research Association Monograph on Curriculum Evaluation, No. 1). Rand McNally, Chicago, 1967.

TABA, H., *Curriculum Development: Theory and Practice*. Harcourt, Brace, New York, 1962.

WISEMAN, S. and PIDGEON, D., *Curriculum Evaluation*. National Foundation for Educational Research, Slough, 1970.

Related general reading

ALBRECHT, M. C., BARNETT, J. H. and GRIFF, M. (eds), *The Sociology of Art and Literature: a Reader*. Duckworth, 1970.

ALVAREZ, A., *The Savage God*. Weidenfeld & Nicolson, 1971.

ANDERSON, JOHN M., *The Realm of Art*. Pennsylvania State University Press, 1967.

ARNHEIM, RUDOLF, *Visual Thinking*. Faber, 1970.

ARNHEIM, RUDOLF, *Toward a Psychology of Art*. University of California Press, 1966/Faber, 1967.

ARNHEIM, RUDOLF, *Art and Visual Perception*. Faber, 1967.

Arts Council of Great Britain (New Activities and the Community Sub-committee), *The Arts and the Community*. Great George's Project, Liverpool, 1970.

BECKET, ERNEST, *The Birth and Death of Meaning*. Free Press of Glencoe, New York, 1962.

BERGSON, HENRI, *Creative Evolution*. Macmillan, 1965.

BERNSTEIN, BASIL, 'On the classification and framing of educational knowledge', in *Knowledge and Control*, ed. M. Young. Collier-Macmillan, 1971.

BERNSTEIN, BASIL, 'Open schools, open society?', *New Society*, 14 September 1967.

BRUNER, JEROME S., *On Knowing – Essays for the Left Hand*. Harvard University Press, 1962.

BRUNER, JEROME S., *The Process of Education*. Harvard University Press, 1966.

BRUNER, JEROME S., *Toward a Theory of Instruction*. Harvard University Press, 1966.

Central Advisory Council for Education (England), *Half our Future* [The Newsom Report]. HMSO, 1963.

COOMBS, P. H., *The World Educational Crisis: a Systems Analysis*. Oxford University Press, New York, 1968.

Department of Education and Science, *Survey of the Curriculum and Deployment of Teachers (Secondary Schools), 1965–66*, Part I: Teachers (Statistics of Education: Special Series No. 1). HMSO, 1968.

DEWEY, JOHN, *Art as Experience*. Minton, Balch, New York, 1934.

DUNCAN, NEIL S., *The Arts in the South: a Preliminary Survey and Report*. Southern Arts Association, 1970.

ECKER, D. W., 'The artistic process as qualitative problem solving', *Journal of Aesthetics and Art Criticism*, **XXI**, spring 1953, 283–90.

EHRENZWEIG, ANTON, *The Hidden Order of Art: Study in the Psychology of Artistic Imagination*. Weidenfeld & Nicolson, 1967.

ERICKSON, R., 'Youth in conflict', *Journal of Secondary Education*, **43**, January 1968, 16–18.

ERICKSON, E. H., *Identity, Youth and Crisis*. Faber, 1971.

Estimates Committee to the House of Commons – Eighth Report, *Grants to the Arts*. HMSO, 1968.

FAGAN, JOEN and SHEPHEARD, IRMA LEE (eds), *Gestalt Therapy Now*. Penguin Books, 1972.

80

FLAVELL, JOHN H., *The Developmental Psychology of Jean Piaget*. Van Nostrand–Reinhold, New York, 1963.

FROMM, ERICH, *The Heart of Man*. Routledge & Kegan Paul, 1965.

GAGNÉ, ROBERT M., *The Conditions of Learning*. Holt, Rinehart & Winston, 1965.

GALLIE, W. B., 'Art as an essentially contested concept', *Philosophical Quarterly*, **6**, 1956, 97–114.

GIEDION, S., *Mechanization Takes Command*. Oxford University Press, New York, 1948.

GOOCH, STAN, *Total Man*. Penguin Books, 1971.

GREEN, MICHAEL and WILDING, MICHAEL, *Cultural Policies in Great Britain*. Unesco, Paris, 1970.

GROPIUS, WALTER, *Apollo in the Democracy: the Cultural Obligation of the Architect*. McGraw-Hill, 1968.

HENDERSON, J. L. and BOLAM, D. W., *Art and Belief*. Hamish Hamilton, 1968.

HIGGINS, JOHN, *Public Patronage of the Arts*. Political and Economic Planning, 1965.

HENRY, JOAN, *Culture Against Man*. Tavistock, 1966.

HIMMELWEIT, H., OPPENHEIM, A. N. and VINCE, P., *Television and the Child*. Oxford University Press, 1958.

HUDSON, LIAM, *Contrary Imaginations: a Psychological Study of the English Schoolboy*. Methuen, 1966.

ILLICH, IVAN, *Deschooling Society*. Calder & Boyars, 1971.

ITTEN, JOHANNES, *Design and Form – the Basic Course at the Bauhaus*. Thames & Hudson, 1964.

JACKSON, BRIAN, *Verdict on the Facts – the Case for Educational Change*. Advisory Centre for Education, Cambridge, 1969.

JONES, RICHARD M., *Fantasy and Feeling in Education*. University of London Press, 1968.

JUNG, C. G., *Memories, Dreams and Reflections*. Collins and Routledge & Kegan Paul, 1963.

KAHLER, E., 'What is art?', in *Problems in Aesthetics*, ed. M. Weitz. Macmillan, New York, 1959.

KANDINSKY, WASSILY, *Concerning the Spiritual in Art*. Wittenborn, New York, 1947.

KEPES, GYORGY, *Language of Vision*. Paul Theobald, 1944.

KEPES, GYORGY, *The New Landscape in Art and Science*. Paul Theobald, 1956.

KEPES, GYORGY, *Structure in Art and Science*. Studio Vista, 1965.

KEPES, GYORGY, *Sign, Image and Symbol*. Studio Vista, 1966.

KEPES, GYORGY, *The Man-made Object*. Studio Vista, 1966.

KETTLE, ARNOLD, *The Artist and Society* (Arts: a Foundation Course (Humanities), Unit 4). Open University Press, 1970.

LAING, R. D. and PHILLIPSON, H., *Interpersonal Perception*. Tavistock, 1966.

LAING, R. D., *The Politics of Experience and the Bird of Paradise*. Penguin Books, 1967.

LAING, R. D., *Self and Others*. Tavistock, 1969.

LANGER, SUZANNE K., *Feeling and Form*. Routledge & Kegan Paul, 1953.

LANGER, SUZANNE K., 'The cultural importance of the arts', in *Aesthetic Form and Education*, ed. M. Andrews. Syracuse University Press, New York, 1958.

LANGER, SUZANNE K., *Philosophy in a New Key*. Harvard University Press, 1957.

LAUWERYS, JOSEPH, *Teachers and Teaching*. Evans, 1969.

LAUWERYS, JOSEPH (ed.), *The World Year Book of Education 1969: Examinations*. Evans, 1969.

LYTTON, HUGH, *Creativity and Education*. Routledge & Kegan Paul, 1971.

MCLUHAN, MARSHALL and PARKER, HARLEY, *Through the Vanishing Point: Space in Poetry and Painting*. Harper & Row, 1969.

MARLAND, MICHAEL, *Towards the New Fifth*. Longman, 1969.

MASLOW, ABRAHAM H., *Motivation and Personality*. Harper & Row, 1970.

MASLOW, ABRAHAM H., *Toward a Psychology of Being*. Van Nostrand–Reinhold, 1968.

MOUSTAKAS, CLARK E. (ed.), *The Self*. Harper & Row, 1956.

MUSGROYE, F., *Patterns of Power and Authority in English Education*. Methuen, 1971.

'Music and art in the public schools', *Art Education*, **XVI**, December 1963, 5–14 (journal of National Art Education Association, Washington).

OSBOREN, HAROLD (ed.), *The Oxford Companion to Art*. Oxford University Press, 1970.

OSBOREN, HAROLD, *The Art of Appreciation*. Oxford University Press, 1970.

PAWLEY, MARTIN, *The Private Future*. Thames & Hudson, 1973.

POLANYI, MICHAEL, *Personal Knowledge*. Routledge & Kegan Paul, 1962.

A Policy for the Arts: the First Steps (Cmnd 2601). HMSO, 1965.

READ, SIR HERBERT, *The Grass Roots of Art*. Faber, 1955.

READ, SIR HERBERT, *The Forms of Things Unknown*. Faber, 1960.

READ, SIR HERBERT, *The Redemption of the Robot: My Encounter with Education through Art*. Trident Press, New York, 1966/Faber, 1970.

READ, SIR HERBERT, *The Meaning of Art*. Pitman, 1951.

REID, LOUIS ARNAUD, *Meaning in the Arts*. Allen & Unwin, 1969.

RICHMOND, KENNETH, *Culture and General Education*. Methuen (University Paperbacks), 1964.

SCHACHTEL, ERNEST G., *Metamorphosis*. Routledge & Kegan Paul, 1963.

Schools Council, *Enquiry 1: Young School Leavers*. HMSO, 1968.

Schools Council, *CSE: a Group Study Approach to Research and Development* (Examinations Bulletin 20). Evans/Methuen Educational, 1970.

SCHOUVALOFF, ALEXANDER (ed.), *Place for the Arts*. North Western Arts Association, Seel House Press, 1970.

SMITH, R. A. (ed.), *Aesthetic Concepts and Education*. University of Illinois Press, 1971.

SPARSHOTT, F. E., *The Structure of Aesthetics*. Routledge & Kegan Paul, 1963.

TAYLOR, L. C., *Resources for Learning*. Penguin Books, 1971.

TUCKER, NICHOLAS, *Understanding the Mass Media*. Cambridge University Press, 1966.

TAYLOR, WILLIAM, *Half a Million Teachers* (Lyndale House Papers). University of Bristol Institute of Education, 1968.

UNESCO, *The Arts and Man: a World View of the Role and Functions of the Arts in Society*. HMSO, 1969.

WEITZ, M. (ed.), *Problems in Aesthetics*. Macmillan, New York, 1959/Collier-Macmillan, 1970.

WHANNEL, P. and HALL, S., *The Popular Arts*. Hutchinson, 1964.

WINNICOTT, D. W., *Playing and Reality*. Tavistock Publications, 1971.

WITKIN, ROBERT W., *The Intelligence of Feeling*. Heinemann Educational, 1974.

WOLLHEIM, RICHARD, *Art and its Objects: Introduction to Aesthetics* (Pelican). Penguin Books, 1970.

Project staff, consultative committee and working party

Project staff (1968–72)

Peter Cox (Director)	Principal, Dartington College of Arts, Totnes, Devon
Malcolm Ross (Organizer)	Seconded from Exeter University Institute of Education to plan, coordinate and administer the work of the project
Robert Witkin (Director of Research)	Seconded from Exeter University Department of Sociology to direct the research programme
Alma Craft (1970–72)	Appointed to assist in gathering data from secondary sources—also compiled bibliography (see Appendix B)
Alison Baker and Colin Vyvyan (1970–71)	Appointed to carry out fieldwork in the six selected schools
Juliet Megee (1971–72)	Appointed to study the therapeutic use of the arts (see Appendix A)
Thames Witkin (1971–72)	Appointed to assist with processing of the data
Margaret Metcalfe (1968–70)	Administrative assistants – appointed to assist with general administration and to compile a detailed
Elizabeth Fyffe (1970–72)	bibliography relating to arts education

Special reports

    Art: Robert Clement, Art Adviser, Education Department, Devon County Council

    Dance: Sue Morris, Head of Dance Department, High School of Art, Manchester

    Curriculum: Jack Walton, Senior Lecturer in Education, Exeter University Institute of Education

Special productions
 The Head by Ed Berman (Inter-Action film)
 'The Life of Feeling', an anthology by John Lane
Valuable assistance was also given to the project by: Gail Bruce, Joan Entwistle, Jane Finnegan, Susan Hine, Margaret Jewell, Alan Lawson, Malcolm and Rosie Orr, Sue Ridler, Ronald Russell, Gill Skinner and Wendy Spall.

Consultative committee

Edward Blacksell (Chairman)	Headmaster, Barnstaple Secondary School, Devon
John Allen	HM Inspectorate (Drama)
Mrs L. Bown	Head of English Department, Fairlop Secondary Girls' School, Essex
Mrs Lucy Burroughs	Head of School of Art Education, Birmingham
Geoffrey W. Cooksey	Joint Secretary, Schools Council
Peter Cox	Principal, Dartington College of Arts, Devon
Professor R. D'Aeth (1971–72)	Acting Director, Institute of Education, University of Exeter
Jack Dobbs	Head of Music Department, Dartington College of Arts, Devon
Walter Drabble	HM Inspectorate (Music)
David Farnell	Head of Art Department, Melbourn Village College, Herts
David Firmstone	Head of Arts Department, Abraham Darby School, Shropshire
Paul Fordham (1968–71)	Project Officer, Schools Council
Dr James Hemming	Psychologist and author
Brian Knight	Headmaster, Holyrood County Secondary School, Chard, Somerset
D. Lilley	Weydon County Secondary School, Farnham (member of Schools Council Arts Committee)
Professor Duncan Mitchell	Head of Department of Sociology, Exeter University
Mrs S. Morris	Head of Dance Department, Manchester High School of Art
Joslyn Owen	Deputy Chief Education Officer, Devon (formerly Joint Secretary, Schools Council)

Ian Parry (1971–72)	Project Officer, Schools Council
Professor Robin Pedley (1968–71)	Director, Institute of Education, University of Exeter
Malcolm Ross	Institute of Education, University of Exeter
Mira Stockl	Postgraduate School of Art Education, Cardiff College of Art
H. R. Wilcock (1971–72)	Principal, West Oxfordshire Technical College
I. Williams (1968–71)	Principal, Thurrock Technical College
Robert Witkin	Sociology Department, University of Exeter

By special invitation

Ed Berman (Project Associate)	Director, Inter-Action Trust, London
Alan Lawson (1968–70)	Secretary, Institute of Education, University of Exeter
Malcolm Orr (1970–72)	Secretary, Institute of Education, University of Exeter
Susan Le Roux	Deputy Publishing Manager, Schools Council

Working party (1967–69)

Peter Cox (Chairman)	Principal, Dartington College of Arts
John Allen	HM Inspectorate (Drama)
Colin Bigwood	King Edward VI School, Totnes, Devon
J. E. Blacksell	Warden, Pilton Community College, Barnstaple
R. Bolsover	Music Adviser, Devon
John Butt	Drama Adviser, Devon
R. Clement	Art Adviser, Devon
J. Dobbs	Dartington College of Arts
Walter Drabble	HM Inspectorate (Music)
Miss Ruth Foster	Dartington College of Arts, Devon
Roy Goddard	Exeter LEA
Geoffrey Harrison	Director, Schools Council Project Technology
Geoffrey Hoare	Department of Education, University of Exeter
Miss Barbara Ingram	Rolle College, Exmouth
B. A. Knight	Headmaster, Chard Secondary School
John Lane	Director, Beaford Centre, N. Devon
Joslyn Owen	Deputy Chief Education Officer, Devon (formerly Joint Secretary, Schools Council)

Stephen Pike   King Edward VI School, Totnes, Devon
Malcolm Ross   Institute of Education, University of Exeter
Fred Smith   St Luke's College, Exeter
Ivor Weeks   Dartington College of Arts, Devon